THE WORLD'S GREATEST

INVESTORS REVEAL THEIR MOST

i

Author's Personal Note

- The ideas in this book were compiled from conversations with the world's greatest investors. Then these same ideas were condensed so that the reader could benefit from all the latest investment strategies and insights currently available.

- The strategies in this book were developed for any unforeseeable economic event that may occur in the future, whether the economy goes straight into a depression, or the politicians finally bring about the golden age of economics.

Attention Computer Users

An easy-to-use software program has been exclusively developed for the IBM and Macintosh computer systems, making it possible for the consumer to utilize the remarkable investment strategies presented in this book. These software programs will be ready to ship in August of 1992. Please send a SASE plus $10 for more information about the software programs and the upcoming newsletter to:

Berkshire Odyssey Investments
2740 Packard Rd. Suite A-31
Ann Arbor, MI 48108

Dear Reader: The current rate for a one-year membership in the Berkshire Odyssey investment club is $10. The investment software program and newsletter are *only available* through Berkshire-Odyssey Investments, with membership only.

Acknowledgments

- Dedicated to my wife, who is my greatest inspiration and lifelong friend.

- S&P Data, Homestake Mining tables, Solomon Brothers, Federal Reserve Data. Various computer programs constructed for this book by the brilliant mathematician Fred Fuld. Concept Studios and Peacock Productions. Shear-Davis International. Mutual fund figures assessed from annual reports then re-assessed by specially developed software programs. Inflation figures are computer verifiable and based on government figures (assuming that the government releases the correct figures). All the investment strategies in this book are solely owned by MNM Publications. Software programs concerning any of these strategies are also owned by MNM Publications.

ISBN 0-9632572-0-X

MNM Publications Phone No. 1-313-973-6262

The strategies in this book are licensable to the general public for private use only. Commercial use of these strategies for monetary gain is strictly prohibited, please send all inquiries to:

Berkshire Odyssey Investments
2740 Packard Rd. Suite A-31
Ann Arbor, MI 48108

The Main Objective Of This Book
Economic survival!

This book was written to achieve two major goals:

No 1. To arm the stock market or income investor with all the information they will need to succeed in the stock, bond, or gold markets.

No 2. To reveal a master trading system that will allow the stock or income investor to profit during any bull or bear market cycle.

Table of Contents

Chapter I
History Constantly Repeats Itself
(At Your Expense)

Author's note: Dear reader, successful investing often begins with the knowledge acquired from a historical review of the past.

What's Up Doc?
Stocks are up you wascally rabbit. Not gold or bonds.

Stocks can make you rich, but it could take a very long-time.

From 1871 to 1992 (121 years), a safe investment in gold or bonds returned less than one percent, (just managing to keep up with inflation). Stocks are a different matter: on average, one dollar invested in 1873 returned $9000 or over 900,000% in 1992.[1]

The Government Makes The Rules,
And The Investor Pays, And Pays, And Pays, And Pays
Uncle Sam owns and operates the biggest numbers game in the world, and only a few people understand the rules.

Never invest in the stock market when its high.

Why?

Take a look at the following example:

If you invested $100,000 in a mutual fund right before the terrible 1973–1974 crash, and the fund broke even in 1977[2], after four years of inflation the original $100,000 would have dropped in value to $73,000. At that point, the investor will have to earn an additional $27,000 or a 38% gain, just to recover from the loss of purchasing power due to inflation.

[The investor must first pay an income tax and a social security tax to receive his/her money; then a capital gains tax on the investment if it makes a profit, plus an invisible tax to inflation; and finally one more tax to break even from the negative side-effects of capital gains taxes and inflation.]

When taxes are added to the above example, the investor will need approximately $142,000 just to break even from the negative side effects of taxes and inflation.

Author's note: Unfortunately, the financial industry often ignores the negative effects of taxes and inflation when they figure the total return of an investment.

---

[1] Stocks were the only investment that beat the negative effects of taxes and inflation during the past 121 years.
[2] Which is precisely what happened to the majority of mutual funds and pension plans during this period.

2 HISTORY CONSTANTLY REPEATS ITSELF AT YOUR EXPENSE

Furthermore, between 1970–1980, a $100,000 investment lost $53,000 to inflation alone:

$100,000 - $53,000 = $47,000

In this scenario, you would need to make approximately 121% on the remaining $47,000 just to break even from inflation.[1]

As a further example (1980–1990), a $100,000 investment lost $38,000 to inflation:

$100,000 - $38,000 = $62,000

Even during the so-called lean Reagan years the investor would have to make an additional 67%, or $45,600, just to recover from the negative effects of taxes and inflation.

The Three Greatest Depressions In U.S. History
Welcome to mortal man's finest achievements!

Somehow the public thinks that their political leaders are the shining examples of man and that they can somehow solve disastrous economic problems – when in reality these men cannot balance their own checkbooks, let alone something as complex as the Federal deficit.[2]

Listed in order of severity:

The biggest crash of the last two centuries started in 1929 and ended in 1942 (commonly known as the Great Depression era). Stocks on average lost 89% of their value during this period.

The Second Great Depression began in the late 1830's. Business output dropped as much as 50% from the previous highs. This depression lasted from 1840–1846.

The third and final depression occurred between 1873–1879. While not as disastrous as the other two, the stock market still managed to lose over 60% of its value during this period.

The 1970's

Most professionals consider the economic losses of the 1970's equal to the losses that occurred during the Great Depression era, since high inflation and excessive taxation wiped out approximately two hundred years of the dollar's value.

The Depressions From 1785 To 1942

Dear Reader: Its time to take a good look at the politician's economic track record during the past 200 years of our nation's history. Please keep these figures in mind the next time you vote.

---

[1] These figures include the adjusted 15% capital gains taxes on the fund, based on the average mixture of short-term and long-term investments.
[2] Some not all.

The Depressions from 1785 to 1942:

1)	The Depression of 1785–1889	15)	The Depression of 1893–1895
2)	The Depression of 1808–1809	16)	The Depression of 1903
3)	The Depression of 1814	17)	The Depression of 1907–1908
4)	The Depression of 1819–1820	18)	The Depression of 1914
5)	The Depression of 1825	19)	The Depression of 1920–1921
6)	The Depression of 1837–1839	20)	The Depression of 1929–1942
7)	The Depression of 1847–1848	21)	Minor Depression in 1798
8)	The Depression of 1857	22)	Minor Depression in 1828–1829
9)	The Depression of 1860–1861	23)	Minor Depression in 1833
10)	The Depression of 1868–1869	24)	Minor Depression in 1882
11)	The Depression of 1873–1875	25)	Minor Depression in 1846
12)	The Depression of 1878	26)	Minor Depression in 1855
13)	The Depression of 1884	27)	Minor Depression in 1882
14)	The Depression of 1889–1890		

This era also included three of the greatest depressions in American history. (*Thank God our politicians know what they're doing!*)

Economic Crashes Between 1794 & 1900
It's never too late to lose your money in the stock market!

1795–1797   Stock market averages lost 26%.

1800–1802   Stock market averages lost 23%.

1805–1806   Stock market averages lost 26%.

1810–1812   Stock market averages lost 20%.

1812–1839   Speculative boom (23 year run up in stock prices), followed by the first Great Depression in American history.

1840–1846   The first Great Depression; stocks lost 70% of their value during this period.

1846–1872   Primary recovery from the first Great Depression. The stock market fully recovers from the first depression then severely crashes again.

1873–1879   Start of the second Great Depression in American history. Stock market averages lost 60%. This depression was commonly referred to as the Panic of 1879. (Duration of crash, six years.)

1879–1893   Speculative boom (14 year run up in stock prices).

1892–1895   Panic of 1983 (stock market averages lost 30%).

1895–1899   Recovery from the Panic of 1893.

For The Reader's Benefit, Here Are All The Depressions, Recessions, And Stock Market Crashes Between 1900 & 1991

Fly the friendly skies of the stock market.

1900   Dow lost 31.9% of its value. (Duration of crash, 1 year.)

1903   Dow lost 37.6% from November 1902 highs to September 1903 lows." (Depression lasted 10 months.)

1907   Dow lost 44%; commonly known as the "Rich Man's Panic of 1907. (Depression ended in 10 months.)

1909   Dow lost 26.3%, beginning in November of 1909 to February 1910. (Bear market ended in 9 months.)

1912   Dow lost 24% and in 1914 the stock market shut down for five months.

1917   Dow lost 40.1%. The crash started in December 1916. The bear market low came in December 1917.

1919   Dow lost 45%. This bear market endured three crash phases before it finally recovered. (Duration 2 years.)

1923   Dow lost 19%. This minor correction was over in 7 months.

1926   Dow lost 17%. This minor correction was over in 2 months.

1929–1932   Dow lost 90%.

                Six big market crashes occurred during this time span:

                September to November 1929, Dow lost 49% in the first phase of the crash.

                The *second* collapse started in April of 1930 through December 1930. The Dow lost 47%.

                The *third* sell-off began in February 1931 and ended in December 1931. The Dow lost an additional 62%.

                The *forth* and final sell-off ended in July of 1932, wiping out the remaining 54% of the Dow's value.

1934   Dow lost 25% of its value in this minor correction. (Duration 10 months.)

1937   Dow lost 49% in thirteen months. This crash occurred even though the economy was improving from the Great Depression.

1940   Dow lost 39% in twenty-eight months. This was the very last phase of the Great Depression era for soon after the war picked up the economy.

1946   Dow lost 24.7% in only four months. Then the market moved

1946, con't.	sideways for three years and tested the lows three times before re-embarking on its biggest upward move of the century.
1953	Dow lost 14%, a minor correction (duration 9 months).
1957	Dow lost 20.7% (high of 522, low of 416) a minor correction (duration 6 months).
1960	Dow lost 18% in this small bear market correction.
1962	Dow lost 30% in just six months (high of 735, a low of 536). This crash lost over 100 million dollars in value, one and a half times as much as the losses that occurred in 1929.
1966	Dow lost 27% in 8 months (high of 995, low of 774). The economy underwent a zero gross national product during this period. Government monetary intervention was becoming a big deciding factor in the marketplace, with higher inflation rates and government spending on the rise.
1968	Dow lost 36% in an extended 31 month downturn. (The stock market hit a high of 985, and a low of 631.) Crash brought on by currency troubles and high interest rates.
1973	Dow lost 45% in 23 months (high of 1052, low of 578). The Mideast oil crisis and the Watergate cover-up sent the stock market to its lowest level in decades.
1977	Dow lost 27% in 17 months (high of 1015, low of 742). Reasons for crash: increasingly higher oil prices and inflationary pressures.
1981	Dow lost 25% (high of 1024, low of 776). Interest rates soared to abnormally high levels, as the Fed made a major attempt to control inflation.
1983	Dow lost 20% (high of 1287, low of 1027). Reasons for crash: an over extended market in technology stocks and higher interest rates.
1987	Dow lost 37% in a speculative buildup that rivaled the roaring 1920's. It was mainly brought on by worries over the budget deficit and excessive stock speculation.
1990	The Dow lost 22% (from a high of 2999, to a low of 2340). The war with Iraq caused a recession, and eight months later the Dow hit a new all time high of 3040.

   Please keep in mind that the above mentioned losses reflect the average decline of well known stocks, such as the Dow, or the Standard's and Poor's 500 Index. Many smaller stocks lose 50% to 70% of their value during an average stock market crash.

   The duration of stock market crashes has varied anywhere between three months to three years, and from the beginning of this century until 1991 the stock market spent nearly 400 months out of 1028 months, or a full 34 years, in bear markets.

Those Wonderfully Rare Stock Market Advances
And their wonderful after-effects.

1812–1835	Speculative boom (23 year run up in stock prices). Followed by the first Great Depression in American history.
1842–1853	Recovery from first Great Depression. The stock market makes it back to its previous high, and then enters the second Great Depression in American history.
1860–1875	Speculative boom (15 year run up in stock prices).
1920–1929	Speculative boom. Followed by the Greatest Depression of all time.
1949–1969	20 years of rising stock prices ends in the two biggest stock market crashes of this century. (Inflation nearly wiped out the dollar's value.)
1975–1992	During this period the United States acquired the greatest level of accumulated debt in recorded history and experienced the biggest banking bail-out of all time.

The Future Outlook ???

Within the next ten to fifteen years the world could experience an economic crisis equal to the Great Depression eras of the past 200 years. Use the investment systems in this book to protect your portfolio from the after-effects of a full scale economic crisis.

Inflation Cycles — Read 'Em And Weep!
Try biting on a loaded bullet—it's less painful than what you're about to read.

The highlighted copy below shows just how much inflation accelerated during and after times of war or military spending.

Study Table I below *very* carefully.

TABLE I

1880–1890 *Deflation* 2% increase $10,000 worth $10250	
1880–1900 Loss of 5% inflation $10,000 worth $9600	
1880–1910 Loss of 15% inflation $10,000 worth $8500	
1880–1920 **Loss** of **60%** inflation $10,000 worth $4000	World War I
1910–1920 **Loss** of **55%** inflation $10,000 worth $4600	World War I
1920–1925 *Deflation* 15% increase $10,000 worth $11,500	
1926–1934 *Deflation* 36% increase $10,000 worth $13,200	
1926–1940 *Deflation* 26% increase $10,000 worth $12,600	
1925–1944 *Deflation* 0% increase $10,000 worth $10,000	
1940–1949 **Loss** of **42%** inflation $10,000 worth $5,800	World War II
1950–1960 Loss of 20% inflation $10,000 worth $8,000	
1940–1960 **Loss** of **53%** inflation $10,000 worth $4,700	World War II
1970–1980 **Loss** of **53%** inflation $10,000 worth $4,700	Defense*
1960–1980 **Loss** of **65%** inflation $10,000 worth $3,500	Defense*
1980–1990 **Loss** of **38%** inflation $10,000 worth $6,200	Defense*
1960–1990 **Loss** of **78%** inflation $10,000 worth $2,200	Defense*
1950–1990 **Loss** of **82%** inflation $10,000 worth $1,800	Defense*

(Defense* – This symbol means "The Arms Race".)

Military spending has always coincided with periods of high inflation. The table on page 6 examines the consequences of military spending, and its effect on the economy.

A Penny Saved Is A Penny Earned
Obviously, Benjamin Franklin never heard of taxes or inflation.

Ever since the 1940's, taxes and inflation have continuously eroded the value of the dollar, eliminating a large portion of the wealth from the middle class. To find out what went wrong, let's take a closer look at the new order that emerged from the rubble of the 1930's, the era commonly known as Keynesian economics. When Keynesian economists tackled the economic woes of the Great Depression era, they more or less concentrated on a few of the problems that caused the great depressions of the past, and ignored the rest. Unfortunately, the very nature of Keynesian economics made it easier for the government to print its way out of trouble than to find a responsible solution to the problem.[1]

Question: What was the biggest problem Keynesian economics failed to address?

Answer: Military spending. One fact any dim-wit is aware of (except the government) is that most wars or defense build-ups bankrupted and destroyed practically every nation on earth during the past five thousand years of recorded history.

Question: What can be done about this problem?

Answer: The government should create its own tax write offs for military expenditures,[2] since modern day weapon systems are usually obsolete within five to ten years after they're built. Think about it: if the average taxpayer is allowed to write off his/her real estate holdings, why isn't the government allowed to write off something as useless as an exploded bomb, or an obsolete weapons system?

During the depression eras of the past (before Keynesian economics), the dollar usually went up in value. For instance, between 1925–1945 (Great Depression era) $10,000 *was still worth* $10,000. However, after Keynesian economics began, the economy experienced countless attacks from high inflation without the beneficial effect of deflation *lowering* prices.

Welcome To The Slave Society Of Tomorrow
You don't have to wait long – it's here today.

No. 1 Ever since Keynesian economics began in the late 1930's, Federal spending continued to increase at alarming levels. Politicians could now spend beyond their wildest dreams (and they did).

---

[1]Historians point out that the continued policy of devaluing the government's currency bankrupted many a nation in the 19th and 20th centuries, especially those that built up massive deficits through excessive defense spending.
[2]Instead of making us pay for it through higher taxes and inflation.

No. 2 Government controls prevented a depression from taking place in the late 1970's. *Unfortunately this created the biggest inflationary losses in our country's history.*

> 1950–1990 Loss of 82% to inflation: $10,000 valued $1,800.

No. 3 Between 1776–1935 (the dollar was worth one dollar).[1] After Keynesian economics began in the late 1930's, over ninety percent of the dollar's value disappeared to government-imposed inflationary policies. (The dollar is presently worth 10 cents.)

No. 4 In the 1990's, the only real growth comes from the debt sector of the economy, since the total combined deficits continually undermine stable economic growth.

Inflation Figures From The Past Forty Years
Brother, can you please spare another dime?
The one I have keeps on shrinking!

> Between 1972–1990 $10,000 fell in value to $3,147. A loss of -68% to inflation.
>
> Between 1962–1980 $10,000 fell in value to $3,668. A loss of -63% to inflation.
>
> Between 1942–1960 $10,000 fell in value to $5,500. A loss of -45% to inflation.
>
> Between 1950–1990 $10,000 fell in value to $1,800. A loss of -82% to inflation.

Carefully Examine The Following

> 1950–1990 Loss of 82% to inflation: $10,000 worth $1,800.

This figure represents the biggest catastrophic loss from inflation in our nation's history.

Keynesian economics failed to address the wasteful government spending that took place from 1950–1990. During this period an extraordinary 82% of the dollar's value disappeared to inflation. If we continue to experience inflation rates as high as 4%–5% during the next 30 to 40 years, then the economy will go through an exact repeat of the 1950–1990 period.[2]

---

[1] Before Keynesian economics began, the dollar often benefited from deflation. For example, between 1925 and 1944, $10,000 was still worth $10,000 because deflation increased the value of the dollar.

[2] Maybe that's what the clever politicians have in mind; what do you think?

It Would Take An Entire Book To Examine
All The Possibilities Of An Economic Depression
Will the politicians save the economy during the 1990's?
Or will they flush it down the toilet, like they have in the past!

No. 1 The new economic figures project the Federal deficit at $5 trillion in 1995, and by the year 2001 the deficit could easily approach the $10 trillion mark.

No. 2 The mounting banking crisis is expected to cost $500 billion to $1 trillion.

No. 3 An alarming number of state and local governments are nearly bankrupt, and their deficits add up to well over $50 billion.

No. 4 A big jump from inflation could easily send interest rates soaring, causing the Federal deficit to expand beyond its already uncontrollable level of growth.

No. 5 Politicians have been promising for more than 30 years to get their heads out of their wazoo's, and find an intelligent answer for lowering the deficit. So far nothing has been accomplished, and probably never will. [Politics (like baseball), is set up in such a way that by the time a good idea gets to first base, the game is already over.]

"I Still Don't Believe The Government Could Ever
End Up In An Economic Crisis"
(Like 1929 or 1973-74)
Then you must be the only person on earth that thinks that way.

The Federal deficit for 1963–1967 was $5.2 billion a year.
The Federal deficit for 1967–1972 was $14 billion a year.
The Federal deficit for 1973–1977 was $39 billion a year.

The Federal deficit for 1991 stands at $364 billion, an increase of over 9 times since 1977. Plus the total Federal debt is projected at $5 trillion in 1995. By the year 2001 the deficit could easily approach the $10 trillion mark.[1]

The Government Never Did Me Any Wrong
Never did me any right, either.

Back in the good old days, 1913 to be exact, taxes had to be paid if you earned one million dollars or more, and only 1/12 of 1 percent of the population paid taxes. However, when Roosevelt came into office, personal income taxes jumped from 1.34% to 18.50%. Furthermore, since 1902, taxes have grown over 30,000 percent.

[1] In addition to all this good news, the Federal deficit along with consumer debt could be as high as $30 trillion within the next ten years. (Depending on the inflation growth rate.)

Is The Stock Market Dead In The United States?
Should you take the few pennies you have left and move on?

During the past 30 years (1960–1990) inflation has averaged five to six percent annually. If this level of inflation continues in the future, it would mean that the stock market will have to return 12% on a compounded basis just to keep up with inflation when it was at the 3.1% annual rate. The figures below show just how much the Dow Jones Industrial Averages will have to grow in order to sustain this level of growth at 1992 levels.

In 2002 (ten years)
it would have to grow to 9,000 or 3 times its present value.

In 2007 (fifteen years)
it would have to grow to 16,000 or 5.3 times its present value.

In 2012 (twenty years)
it would have to grow to 28,000 or 9.3 times its original value.

In 2017 (twenty five years)
it would have to grow to 51,000 or 17 times its original value.

In 2022 (thirty years)
it would have to grow to 89,000 or 29.6 times its original value.

It's Time To Find Out How Much The Gains And Losses For The Dow Jones Industrial Averages Have Been Since 1885
The secret's out! I bet your broker, financial advisor,
or hot-to-trot financial newsletter doesn't want you to know about this!

In order of importance, here are *all* the percentage gains needed for the Dow to break even after each of the bear markets crashes since 1886.

PART 1

1886	(25%)	1912	(31%)	1937	(100%)	1969	(67%)
1892	(75%)	1917	(66%)	1940	(65%)	1973	(82%)
1896	(33%)	1919	(83%)	1946	(34%)	1977	(38%)
1900	(47%)	1923	(23%)	1953	(17%)	1981	(34%)
1903	(61%)	1926	(21%)	1960	(23%)	1983	(25%)
1907	(76%)	1929	(900%)	1962	(42%)	1987	(60%)
1909	(36%)	1934	(34%)	1966	(38%)	1990	(28%)

PART 2
The above figures were then processed in a high-speed computer, in order to find out where the most profitable area of compounding takes place in the stock market:

From 1900 To 1991 Dow Gained 234000% Lost 10 Million Percent
From 1909 To 1991 Dow Gained 139000% Lost 2.4 Million Percent
From 1919 To 1991 S&P Gained 73500% Lost 818 Thousand Percent
From 1925 To 1991 S&P Gained 36000% Lost 300 Thousand Percent

From 1934 To 1991 S&P   Gained 41000%   Lost 30 Thousand Percent
From 1940 To 1991 S&P   Gained 25000%   Lost 11.1 Thousand Percent
From 1950 To 1991 Dow   Gained 10000%   Lost 5 Thousand Percent
From 1960 To 1991 Dow   Gained 1700%   Lost 3.3 Thousand Percent
From 1969 To 1991 Dow   Gained   700%   Lost 1.3 Thousand Percent
From 1973 To 1991 Dow   Gained   500%   Lost 763 Percent
From 1980 To 1991 Dow   Gained   380%   Lost 245 Percent
From 1984 To 1991 Dow   Gained   150%   Lost 157 Percent

PART 3

The average bottom of a bear market is closer than you think. Thanks to computer technology, we can easily find out where the bottom occurs.[1]

Here Are The Average Lows For All The Bear Markets During The 20th Century

Buying into the stock market any time you feel like it is like jumping out of an airplane—without a parachute.

The figures above and below will show the reader just how important it is to invest in a bear market, since this is the only way the investor will be able to compound his/her investment capital faster than the losses that occur from taxes and inflation.

Take a look at the following figures. Historically, the start of any bull market begins at the -29% level.

1900 To 1991   Average Bear Bottom   -32 Percent Drop
1910 To 1991   Average Bear Bottom   -31 Percent Drop
1919 To 1991   Average Bear Bottom   -31 Percent Drop
1929 To 1991   Average Bear Bottom   -32 Percent Drop
1934 To 1991   Average Bear Bottom   -29 Percent Drop
1940 To 1991   Average Bear Bottom   -28 Percent Drop
1950 To 1991   Average Bear Bottom   -27 Percent Drop
1960 To 1991   Average Bear Bottom   -29 Percent Drop
1969 To 1991   Average Bear Bottom   -30 Percent Drop
1973 To 1991   Average Bear Bottom   -29 Percent Drop
1980 To 1991   Average Bear Bottom   -27 Percent Drop

Since the computer does not lie, why are all the so-called top investment advisors constantly *urging* you to buy when the market is high? Elementary, my dear investor: either they don't know what they're doing (doubtful), or they're *after* your money. The real bull market starts anywhere between minus 17% to minus 30% from the previous all-time high.

---

[1]From 1900 to 1991.

THE DREADED "WALL OF WORRY" SYNDROME

Hey, Mom, Rip Van Winkle just woke up after twenty years—
and the Dow Jones Industrial Averages still hasn't moved one point!

When the stock market returns to its former high (after a crash) it experiences a condition known as the dreaded wall of worry. Investors and institutional managers stay on the sidelines because they realize that the stock markets earnings ratios are high in relation to future economic projections.

Table III shows just how hard it is for the Dow to advance beyond its former high.

TABLE III

Crash of 1929 to 1932	Dow high	381 Low	41	Loss 89%
Crash of 1934	Dow high	110 Low	85	Loss 25%
Crash of 1937	Dow high	194 Low	99	Loss 49%
Crash of 1940 to 1942	Dow high	155 Low	93	Loss 39%
Crash of 1946	Dow high	212 Low	163	Loss 25%
Crash of 1957	Dow high	520 Low	419	Loss 21%
Crash of 1960	Dow high	685 Low	566	Loss 18%
Crash of 1961 to 1962	Dow high	734 Low	535	Loss 27%
Crash of 1966	Dow high	995 Low	744	Loss 25%
Crash of 1969 to 1970	Dow high	985 Low	631	Loss 36%
Crash of 1973 to 1974	Dow high	1052 Low	578	Loss 45%
Crash of 1977	Dow high	1015 Low	742	Loss 27%
Crash of 1981	Dow high	1024 Low	776	Loss 21%
Crash of 1983	Dow high	1287 Low	1027	Loss 20%
Crash of 1987	Dow high	2722 Low	1739	Loss 36%
Crash of 1990	Dow high	2999 Low	2340	Loss 22%

- From a high of 381 in October 1929 to the next high of 381 in 1954, the Dow Jones Industrial Averages took 25 years to break even.

- From the lows of 1929 the Dow took 7 years to break even.

- From the highs in 1938 the Dow took another 7 years to break even.

- From 1954 to 1964 the Dow merely doubled in 10 years.

- From 1956 (Dow 500) to 1972 (Dow 1000) the Dow merely doubled in 16 years.

- From 1964 (Dow 800) to 1985 (Dow 1500) the Dow nearly doubled in 21 years.

- From 1972 (Dow 1000) to 1987 (Dow 2000) the Dow merely doubled in fifteen years.

Recovery, Recovery, Where For Art Thou, Recovery?
When a double dip is NOT a double-dip.

Economists now believe that the recession is over (as of January 1992). They further contend that stronger economic growth will return to every sector of the economy. Unfortunately, this could be the very first phase of the current recession, for during the last five recessions the economy fell right back into a double-dip recession.[1]

Beware Of False Financial Gods
They've all been kicked out of Hell, for
God decided it wasn't hot enough for them!

Every time the stock market reaches new highs, books and newspaper articles come out with the latest financial scams aimed at the small investor. These periodicals constantly urge the investor to get into the market right away. What they don't explain to you is that waiting for a bear market can easily add up to 2.8% to your portfolio's long-term performance record.

The average return for the past ten years has been 11.2%.

The figures below have been adjusted for the added 2.8% gain on a $10,000 investment:

15 Years at:	11.2%	=	49,155 Dollars
15 Years at:	14%	=	71,379 Dollars
20 Years at:	11.2%	=	83,578 Dollars
20 Years at:	14%	=	137,434 Dollars
25 Years at:	11.2%	=	142,108 Dollars
25 Years at:	14%	=	264,619 Dollars
30 Years at:	11.2%	=	241,625 Dollars
30 Years at:	14%	=	509.501 Dollars
35 Years at:	11.2%	=	410,835 Dollars
35 Years at:	14 %	=	981,000 Dollars
40 Years at:	11.2%	=	698,540 Dollars
40 Years at:	14%	=	1,888,835 Dollars
50 Years at:	11,2%	=	2,702,942 Dollars
50 Years at:	14%	=	11,000,000 Dollars

As you can see, a few percentage points can dramatically increase the short or long term performance of your investments.

---

[1] The last five out of eight recessions. A double-dip recession means the stock market and the economy fall right back into a deeper recession.

An Incredibly Thoughtless Thing To Say
No, we're not talking about politicians!

Have you ever heard a Wall Street professional say, "If you find good value (meaning, a stock or a bond, with strong fundamental values) then don't worry about the stock market's price when you purchase it." Nothing could be further from the truth, for if the investment was a good buy when the stock market is high, then it should be an outstanding investment after the Dow loses 17% or more of its value. The unfortunate investor who buys near the middle or high of the markets price range may have to wait years in order to recover from the adverse effects of taxes, inflation, and financial fees.

Can Stocks Become Overpriced Like Merchandise?
Only if you pay more than they're worth – which is about two cents.

A brief explanation:

PE's, or Price Earnings ratios, often reflect the price of a company's earnings in relation to its prominence in a particular industry. If earnings are accelerating, then PE ratios will rise to reflect this increase.[1] However, if earnings are declining, then PE ratios will eventually fall. Consequently, *extreme caution* should be observed when PE's are near or at their historic highs, since many of the largest stock market crashes in history have occurred during these periods. In contrast, when PE's are rapidly falling, the market as a whole becomes undervalued, and an upward surge in prices soon follows.

Financial Yo-Yo's
Send in the clowns!

In 1987, several well-known financial advisors admitted that the stock market was trading at extremely high levels.

Question: Then why didn't these pros instruct their clients to sell, before the crash?

Answer: Elementary, my dear investor; they were all too concerned about next year's earnings projections to notice the dangerous events taking place. Top *institutional analysts*[2] everywhere agreed that economic growth would eventually pick up enough momentum to justify the historically high PE ratios of stocks. Unfortunately, *institutional analysts* are never going to admit the market is overvalued, even if the Dow goes to 9 trillion. Why? Because they make their biggest commissions in roaring bull markets. That's why!!!

---

[1] Good news or bad news about a company may also affect the stock's price, even though earnings still remain favorable.
[2] Some but not all of the institutional analysts that work for large financial firms.

Why Do The Best Laid Plans Of Mice Or Men Fail?
Maybe it's because they were written by rats!

Why do most investors fail in the stock market?

No. 1   *Investors often switch into and out of their favorite investment a hundred times a year,* making their brokers richer and themselves poorer.

No. 2   *Most investors follow the actions of the crowd or the popular opinion.* This is one of the *surest* ways to become a loser in the financial markets. Witness the real estate crash of the 1990's, or the twenty-six stock market crashes of this century; the huge gold market crash of 1979, or the 50% loss in real estate values during the Great Depression era. *Remember, each of these areas of the economy were unanimously followed by the popular opinion.*

No. 3   *Wave theories.* These new-age theories can be interpreted from so many different *points of view* that the investor can never be assured of their accuracy.

Some People Are Totally Out Of Touch With Reality!

At the brink of the greatest stock market crash in history, Calvin Coolidge was quoted at saying, "Everything is absolutely sound with the economy, and stocks are cheap at their current price levels."

After crashing more than 1000 points in 1987, Ronald Reagan said, "I can't understand why the stock market fell so much. There's absolutely nothing wrong with the economy."

The most famous economists are often asked how the stock market or economy will perform during the next year. Over 95% of their predictions are wrong.[1]

Studies from the 1960's show that monkeys throwing darts at the stock section of a newspaper can easily outperform 95% of Wall Street's highest paid investment advisors.

Last Remarks: Get yourself a monkey and teach him how to throw darts.

Author's personal note: If you made it this far, then you may have what it takes to become a successful investor.

---

[1] Over the long haul.

Chapter II
Mutual Funds and Reality

Who Wins, You Or The Government?
Guess!

Dear Reader: Uncle Sam has changed all the rules for the long-term investor during the past thirty years. For example, if you invested $10,000 back in 1959, your investment would have grown into $190,000 in 1992. Unfortunately, when the losses from taxes and inflation have been deducted, a $10,000 investment actually returned $35,000, or two-and-a-half times the original investment.[1] *(The government was the big winner during this period, not you.)*

As a further example: A $10,000 investment in a mutual fund back in 1967 grew to an average sum of $110,000 in 1990. Unfortunately, when the effects of taxation and inflation have been deducted, $80,000 of this amount disappeared into Uncle Sam's pocket. (Remember, it took a $45,000 investment in 1991 to equal a $10,000 investment back in 1965.) So if the mutual fund returned $90,000 on a $10,000 investment, it merely doubled.[1]

Since $45,000 equaled $10,000 in 1965, we figure:

$45,000 x 2 = $90,000 (this equaled $20,000 back in 1965).

In 25 years the average mutual fund investment merely doubled. As you can see, the government can easily take up to 90% of the profit from your investment, *especially* if you choose to invest at the wrong time.

Historically Speaking, When Should I Consider Investing?
You mean with honest Uncle Sam running the government? Never!

Question: How can the investor make a profit with Uncle Sam around?

Answer: Simple. Invest in a severe stock market crash, when small stocks lose 55% to 70% of their value. During market crashes such as these, *i.e.*, 1973–1974 or 1969–1970, small cap mutual funds became so undervalued that many of them doubled or even tripled the return of the average mutual fund throughout this period (1975–1992).

Question: How much could I make or lose investing at the wrong time?

Answer: If you invested $10,000 in a typical small stock fund back in 1975, your investment probably returned between $180,000–$300,000 in 1990. *[Then after taxes and inflation have been deducted, the previous amount will have dropped in value to $50,000–$100,000].* Now a return this large usually takes thirty five to forty years to achieve. However, because the investor was patient enough to buy into a severe crash, he/she received fifteen to twenty years of additional compounding free!

---

[1]This figure was based on the averages, and tax consequences are either greater or lesser than the above figure. In other words, Uncle Sam was the big winner in the investment arena, not you.

Different scenario: This time the amateur investor waits until the market recovers before he/she makes an investment. Later in 1990 that investment will have returned (on average) between $90,000–$130,000. *[Unfortunately, after taxes and inflation have been deducted, the previous amount will drop in value to $25,000–$30,000 in 1990 dollars (or one to two times the original investment.)]* So by waiting an additional year for the market to recover, the amateur investor unknowingly threw away twenty years of free compounding.

Since it takes a severe crash to accumulate greater than average returns in the stock market, the investor should sit back and wait for small stock mutual funds to lose 50% to 60% of their value. Then invest.

The international investor is also in a good position to take advantage of strong economies (i.e., Japan, Germany, etc.) that have undergone severe stock market crashes.

When They're Hot, They're Hot
When they're not, you profit.

When you select a mutual fund in a bear market, always check the hardest hit small cap funds first.[1] The greater the fund's losses are in a crash, the better the return will be when the stock market eventually recovers. In many cases the biggest losers are often the star performers in the prior bull market, since they typically fall twice as fast as the Dow or the S&P 500 during a crash.

The nine criterion for picking a good small stock fund are as follows:

No. 1 Make sure the fund stays away from speculative investment techniques, such as options, futures, or margin.

No. 2 Look for a small cap fund or a number of sector funds that were the best performers in the bull market prior to the crash. Why? Aggressive funds are often among the biggest losers in a bear market, and the *biggest winners* during the recovery.

No. 3 The fund is well diversified among 8 to 10 industry groups.

No. 4 The fund doesn't charge a big sales fee to get in.

No. 5 The fund has an outstanding long-term performance record, including the most recent five year period.

No. 6 The same superstar manager is running the fund.

No. 7 Check out the Forbes Honor Roll list. If the fund is rated A or A+ in up markets, and C or D in down markets, then it has a good chance of making larger than average gains during a recovery.

No. 8 When you invest in an international fund, make sure that the country or countries are politically and economically stable.

---

[1]Again, make sure they don't use margin or other speculative investment techniques.

No. 9 Make sure that the fund turns over its portfolio *slowly,* since this will produce favorable long-term tax benefits and a greater return on your investment.[1]

I'm Hard Hit!
Does this mean I'm a winner?

Question: Why should I look at the hardest hit areas of the economy during a crash?

Answer: If a mutual fund or sector-fund is concentrated in the hardest hit industrial groups during a crash, then the stocks in these funds will usually outperform the averages in the subsequent recovery. Pay special attention to areas of the economy that are recession sensitive and always bounce back after a recession. (These areas include technology, automotive, computers, banking, retailing, construction, consumer products, insurance, health care, etc.)

When A Small Stock Mutual Fund Isn't Small Anymore
The incredible shrinking return.

When you choose a small stock fund, make sure its total assets are under $200 million. Why? When a mutual fund becomes larger in size it must eventually add larger company stocks to its portfolio. At that point it can no longer limit its investments to smaller company stocks.

What About A Mutual Fund That Uses Margin?

Never buy a fund that purchases stocks on margin. In the 1930's a large number of closed-end funds were wiped out because of excessive margin trading. Stay diversified and margin free and make sure that your mutual fund has the same investment policy.

The Biggest Mistakes Amateur Or Professional Investors Make

No. 1 Most investors believe they can get ahead of Uncle Sam by investing in dollar cost averaging plans. Unfortunately, the newest research findings point out that it takes a full fledged crash for compounding to dramatically outpace the losses that occur from taxes and inflation.

No. 2 Most mutual funds either charge too much for their expense fees or underperform the market averages as a whole.

No. 3 Watch out for bond funds; these funds charge excessively high expense fees.

---

[1]Assuming that the government ever brings back favorable long-term capital gains tax write-offs.

No. 4 Index funds (like the S&P 500) typically outperform 90% of all mutual funds.

No. 5 Keep away from up-front sales loads, back-in loads, or 12-B1 fees, coupled with high annual expense fees.

No. 6 Avoid the hottest growth fund when the stock market is up. Only purchase these funds at the bottom of a severe crash, since they have the most to gain during the recovery.

No. 7 Find a mutual fund with an outstanding long-term performance record.

No. 8 Switch out of the fund that has changed its investment policy, or is currently under new management.

No. 9 Stay away from new funds until they've had a chance to prove themselves. Avoid spin-off funds with the same name or a different manager.

I See Top Performing Mutual Funds Everywhere
Dear Reader: Do you remember the old saying: "Here one minute, gone the next?"

Look at the long-term performance record for any of the best mutual funds during the past five-, ten-, or twenty-year periods. You will find that only a very few funds manage to remain on the top performing list for any length of time.

Question: Why does this occur?

Answer: Because very few investment strategies work in changing economic environments. And many of the best performing mutual funds remain fully invested when the market approaches extremely over-valued levels.

Question: Why would anyone want to remain fully invested when the market is that high?

Answer: Because this will create the biggest percentage gain for the fund before the market crashes, causing a flood of new investment money to pour into the fund, thereby making the mutual fund manager and his financial institution an incredible amount of money in a short period of time.

The Dollar Cost Averaging Scam
The word "average" means exactly what it says.
The investor can never hope to do better than the average.

During this century the stock market has advanced 65% of the time, and declined 35% of the time.

This means the typical dollar cost averaging plan buys too many shares when the market is up, and not enough shares when the market is down. For example, let's say that you invest in a monthly dollar cost averaging plan. Now, it doesn't matter whether the stock market goes straight up or straight down. You're simply paying to much for those shares in the long run.

Ask yourself this question: *What kind of chance do I have succeeding in the financial markets when I invest the same way everyone else does?* [1]

The Answer: Zero!

Is There Any Significant Advantage To Owning More Than Two Mutual Funds?

No. Mutual funds are so diversified that owning more than two funds is often no better than owning an index fund. Computer testing reveals that the odds of doing better than the averages are substantially reduced when the investor owns more than two mutual funds. Sector funds are a different matter if the investor purchases the hardest hit sector funds in a crash and waits until they've fully recovered. Then owning three or four funds often lessens the market risk associated with those particular industries.

Are Gold Mutual Funds Profitable During An Economic Crisis?
Only if you use the gold system in this book.

No. 1   In the 1920's stocks were making enormous returns. Then, during the 1930's, the stock market severely crashed, erasing all of the gains of the prior decade. (Gold stocks were the only sector of the economy that made astonishing returns of 500% or more.)

No. 2   When the inflationary policies of the 1970's shattered the stock market and much of the economy, gold mutual funds once again soared to record breaking levels. (According to Solomon Brothers, gold achieved an astounding 31.9% compounded return in the 1970's.)

Author's note: Unfortunately, the gold market was so volatile during this period only a few investors managed to make enough profit to offset the losses in their stock or bond portfolios.

In answer to the first question: are gold mutual funds or stocks really worth owning during an economic crisis? Yes; just remember to use the special gold trading system in Chapter V. This unique trading system was designed to profit from the extreme volatility of the gold market.

Why Will Smaller Countries (And Their Stock Markets) Continue To Lead The Way In Economic Growth?
Boom-Boom! Bang-Bang!
I've got more nuclear weapons than you. That's why!

---

[1] Through the use of dollar cost averaging plans.

Fact: The United States and Russia spend enormous amounts of capital on defense systems. As a result, massive deficits continually undermine and stall economic growth. Consequently, smaller countries see this as the unique opportunity to expand their markets since there's little the Superpowers can do to regain their former economic superiority.

The First Time I Saw My
Mutual Funds Expense Fees I Nearly Fainted

Doesn't it seem kind of strange that you hand over $10,000, and then they take back over $100,000? Maybe they work for the government?

Dear Reader: If you let your mutual fund assault you with excessive expense fees, forget about retirement and start thinking about being homeless at age sixty-five. Some mutual funds charge as much as two percent or more on an annual basis. While this may not sound excessive to most people, a two-percent expense fee can easily wipe out your entire financial future, as Table IV on the next page reveals.

Fees, Fees, Fees, And More Fees,
What More Do They Want From Me?

Just your soul, that's all!

It's a license to steal time. First there were widespread insurance scams, then credit card interest rate rip-offs, and now, last but not least, mutual funds and their excessive expense fees.

Expense Fees

A computer was used to compare the compounded losses that occurred during each investment period to what the investor could have gained with or without expense fees.

Example: A 35-year investment return compounded at 10.2% equals $299,471. After deducting the annual 2.1% expense fee, this investment will lose approximately $146,700 of its value. *Nearly half of your entire profit disappeared to expense fees!* And, this figure does not include taxes or inflation.

Losses To Expense Fees On A $10,000 Investment

The total return (not including taxes or inflation) from a 10.2% compounded annual rate is stated in Table IV. The symbol for total return has been highlighted.

TABLE IV

Total Return At 10.2% Compounded	For 10 Years $26,412	For 20 Years $69,764	For 35 Years $299,471
After Yearly Expense Fees	For 10 Years	For 20 Years	For 35 Years
0.42 %	$1,000 Loss	$5,100 Loss	$37,500 Loss
1.0 %	$2,300 Loss	$11,600 Loss	$81,800 Loss
1.5 %	$3,400 Loss	$16,700 Loss	$114,100 Loss
1.8 %	$4,000 Loss	$19,600 Loss	$131,200 Loss
2.1 %	$4,600 Loss	$22,300 Loss	$146,700 Loss
2.5 %	$5,400 Loss	$25,700 Loss	$165,300 Loss
3.0 %	$6,400 Loss	$29,600 Loss	$185,500 Loss
3.5 %	$7,300 Loss	$33,200 Loss	$202,700 Loss
4.0 %	$8,100 Loss	$36,500 Loss	$217,400 Loss

Expense fees above one percent can take a big bite out of your fund's total return. The longer you stay in a fund with fees over one percent, the more devastating the long-term results.

Losses To Expense Fees On A $10,000 Investment

Choose a money market or income fund *with extreme caution.* Many of these funds have *excessively* high expense fees. The next section again compares the compounded losses that occurred during each investment period to what the investor could have gained with or without expense fees.

The total return (not including taxes or inflation) at a 6% compounded annual rate. The symbol for total return has been highlighted.

TABLE V

Total Return At 6% Compounded	For 10 Years $17,908	For 20 Years $32,071	For 35 Years $102,857
After Yearly Expense Fees	For 10 Years	For 20 Years	For 35 Years
0.42 %	$700 Loss	$2,400 Loss	$15,000 Loss
1.0 %	$1,620 Loss	$5,500 Loss	$32,400 Loss
1.5 %	$2,400 Loss	$7,900 Loss	$44,700 Loss
1.8 %	$2,800 Loss	$9,300 Loss	$51,000 Loss
2.1 %	$3,248 Loss	$10,578 Loss	$56,600 Loss
2.5 %	$3,800 Loss	$12,200 Loss	$63,300 Loss
3.0 %	$4,500 Loss	$14,000 Loss	$70,200 Loss
3.5 %	$5,100 Loss	$16,700 Loss	$76,000 Loss

Review the table on the bottom of page 23. A 1.8% expense fee for 35 years *will consume nearly half of the return from your investment.*

Vanguard Group Of Funds • 1-800-662-7447

The Vanguard mutual fund group has a policy of keeping fees as low as possible. Fees for their funds range anywhere between 0.20% to 0.40% of one percent. The *lowest* in the world!

Bargain Hunter's Alert:

Pay special attention to the Vanguard small cap fund. This fund concentrates its portfolio on the small cap stocks of the Russell 2000 index. From October 1990 to March 1991, this fund was up 45%, making it one of the top performers of all funds during this period.

The Fidelity Funds • 1-800-544-8888

Their low expense fees are as follows:

Fidelity Equity Income	(0.70%)
Fidelity Low Priced Stock Fund	(0.80%)
Fidelity Puritan	(0.65%)
Fidelity Trend	(0.61%)
Fidelity Spartan Market Index	(0.28%)

The World's Greatest Investor's Top Choices For The 1990's And Beyond
Once again it's Super Lotto time.

If the reader skipped every other chapter just to read this section, then he/she completely missed the whole point of this book. For the investor who looks at the past performance of a mutual fund or stock sees just that: *the past; not the future.* Please go back and re-read everything in this book over and over again until you fully understand it. *(Remember that this book was written to elevate the investor beyond the average understanding of the market place, and to provide him/her with the investment strategies to do so.)*

It's Time For The Super-Lotto Drawing Of The Century
And the winners are:

The long-time favorite choice among top investors has always been Berkshire Hathaway. This company is currently owned and operated by two of the world's finest investors (Warren Buffett and Charles Munger). The symbol is **Brk** on the New York Stock Exchange. This investment team returned over 74000%, or 740 times the original investment, in a mere twenty-five year period. An astounding return unmatched in the annals of portfolio management.

A Primary List Of The Funds That Achieved The
Greatest Returns During The Past 16 Years
Between 1975 lows to 1991.[1]

Twentieth Century Growth: $10,000 grew into $380,000
Twentieth Century Select: $10,000 grew into $350,000
Acorn Fund: $10,000 grew into $240,000
Alliance Quasar Fund: $10,000 grew into $310,000
Evergreen Fund: $10,000 grew into $305,000
Mathers Fund: $10,000 grew into $210,000
Pennsylvania Mutual Fund: $10,000 grew into $360,000
Sequoia Fund: $10,000 grew into $330,000
Value Line Leveraged Growth: $10,000 grew into $280,000
Fidelity Destiny Portfolio-Destiny I: $10,000 grew into $290,000
Lindner Fund: $10,000 grew into $350,000
Nicholas Fund: $10,000 grew into $240,000
Mutual Shares: $10,000 grew into $250,000

Phone Numbers for Above Funds

Twentieth Century Mutual Funds, 1-800-345-2021
Quasar Alliance Fund, 1-800-221-5672
Evergreen Fund, 1-800-235-0064
Mathers Fund, 1-800-962-3863
Pennsylvania Mutual Fund, 1-800-221-4268
Value Line Leveraged Growth Fund, 1-800-223-0818
Fidelity Destiny Portfolio Fund, 1-800-544-8888
Lindner Fund, 1-314-727-5305
Nicholas Fund, 1-800-227-5987
Mutual Shares Fund, 1-800-448-3863

Look for three or four unrelated fidelity sector funds that have lost a great deal in a crash; or a foreign fund that concentrates its portfolio on severely undervalued stocks, such as the Japan Fund, 1-800-53-JAPAN.

Author's personal note:

Ok reader's, I know you've been waiting a long time for this moment so without any further interruption, its time to reveal the best-performing mutual fund for the next twenty years.

Unfortunately, my mother taught me *not* to lie.[2] So if you want to use the most successful investment strategy of the last 20 years, you could try the following example. I use it all the time and it has never failed me once. Honest!

Studies from the 1960's show that monkeys throwing darts at the stock section of a newspaper can easily outperform 95% of Wall Street's highest paid investment advisors.

[1]Approximate returns.
[2]Like a politician.

Last Remarks:

Get yourself a monkey, teach him how to throw darts. Then use the previous page as a dart board.

Serious Last Remarks: Follow the investment strategies in Chapter V.

By the way, my monkey picked Berkshire Hathaway, the Twentieth Century Growth Fund, the Acorn Fund, the Sequoia Fund, Mutual Beacon and the Pennsylvania Mutual Fund. (Maybe he was having a good day!)

Chapter III
The World's Greatest Investment Tips

Author's Personal Note:

Do you remember the song "There must be 50 ways to leave your lover" by Paul Simon? Well, there must be 50,000 ways to lose your money in the stock, bond, or gold markets. This book avoids the 49,998 ways that don't work, and concentrates on the very few that do. The following is a short list of things to avoid, if you really want financial happiness.

No. 1   Never lend money to friends or relatives. It rarely works out, and if it does, it isn't worth the trouble. (You can usually make a better deal with the devil.)

No. 2   Learn enough about the various financial markets to make your own decisions.

No. 3   Never invest in the stock, bond, or gold market unless you can *easily* withstand a severe crash.

No. 4   Never panic in a stock, bond, or gold market crash. Follow the systems in this book and look forward to market crashes instead of fearing them. If you can't learn to accept this principle, then stay away from the financial markets entirely.

No. 5   Develop the knowledge and wisdom it takes to succeed in the market. Formulate a plan of action that will help you get through the toughest economic times. (Pay special attention to the strategies in Chapter V.)

No. 6   When a broker or financial advisor offers any kind of investment advice *(be careful)*, ask him to provide you with all the information that is currently available. Then do some further investigation on your own.

No. 7   Find out how much mutual funds and other financial institutions charge on an annual basis. Re-read the paragraph in Chapter II titled, "Expense Fees."

No. 8   Avoid financial seminars from slick-rick salesmen. These con artists constantly wow the public with their expensive boats, big houses, and massive banks accounts. What they don't tell you is that they make the majority of their wealth from the people that sign up to expensive seminars, not by successfully investing their money in real estate, stocks, bonds, or gold. Now I'm sure there are a few lucky people (maybe one in a million) who do get rich by being in the right place at the right time. However, don't attend investment seminars based on a one-in-a-million chance for success. Your retirement fund is far too important for this kind of nonsense.

No. 9   Never assume that politicians are capable of doing anything right. The
political breed has two functions, and two functions only: to buy your
vote, and to stay in office. [The less said about these clowns the
better.]

The Greatest Investors Know The One Secret
To Successful Stock Market Investing

And the secret is: *You cannot make a profit in the stock market unless you
develop the attitude to invest in a crash*, since unpredictable inflation and
taxation often eliminates most of the profit at the middle or top of the market's
price range.

People Speculate On Far Too Many Things
May I speculate on your speculation?

Why do so many investors fail in the stock, bond, or gold markets?

No. 1   They follow the advice of professionals who recommend dangerous
investment strategies, such as stock market margin, options on
futures, commodity trading, penny stocks, or shorting techniques.

No. 2   They listen to some of the analysts employed at Wall Street firms.
These people will say it's a good time to invest when every stock on
the N.Y.S.E. has filed for bankruptcy.

No. 3   They refuse to invest in a major market crash.

No. 4   They follow the advice of people who know less than they do.

No. 5   They have no aptitude for the stock market, and should stay out of the
financial markets entirely.

If You Can't Beat 'Em, Join 'Em
Right, Warren?

Warren Buffett is well known in financial circles as the greatest investor of
all time. If the economy ever slips into a severe recession or depression, his
advice could turn out to be extremely helpful in locating severely undervalued
stocks or bonds. If you don't know who Warren Buffett is, a few magazine
articles will introduce you to the man and his unique investment philosophies.

- *Esquire Magazine* Article On Buffett, October 1988 (Page 103)
  This magazine article reveals many of his best known investment
  strategies.
- *Fortune Magazine* Article April 11, 1988 (Page 26)
- *Fortune Magazine* Article November 5, 1990 (Page 27)
- *Business Week* Article September 4, 1989 (Page 9)

There is also a very good section on Warren Buffett in John Train's best-selling book, *The Money Masters,* published by Penguin Books.

Words Of Wisdom From The Greatest Investors Of All Time

No. 1   If the prices on the stock, bond, or gold exchanges drop to a ten or twenty year low. Every dollar that you invest in the market will be at least ten to twenty years *ahead* of the markets price range. Consequently, every dollar that you sell will be at least ten to twenty years *behind* the markets price range.

No. 2   The greatest area of economic growth will come from those countries with the highest savings rates. The lowest areas of growth will come from the countries with the lowest savings rates. In other words, no savings, no growth.

No. 3   Show me a government that encourages investment in its own country, and I'll show you the next economic leader. Japan is the perfect example: they have the highest savings rate in the world, and the lowest inflation (2% per annum). In contrast, the United States has the highest tax rates on capital gains in the world, with an annual inflation rate between 4% to 6%.

No. 4   Show me a government that doesn't work with its people to encourage savings and I'll show you the world's next has-been. For example, the Taiwanese government recently imposed capital gain taxes on investments. Consequently, their stock market crashed 70% from its high. (Taxes and inflation are damaging to economic growth; look at the United States.)

No. 5   When you buy the same stock everyone else is buying, you stand to make very little. However, if you buy the most promising stocks in the hardest hit industries, you stand to make a great deal of money.

No. 6   A contrarian investor will always look at the stocks no one else wants. The stocks your broker might say, "God, no! Do you actually want to own that dog?" If the company's balance sheet is strong, and the future outlook of the company is bright, what more could you ask for?

No. 7   Always check on what the greatest master investors are buying, since their ideas are worth checking into. *Just remember that they make mistakes like anyone else.*

No. 8   If a company's sales have been rising sharply, do some further investigation on your own. Maybe they've come up with a unique product or service everyone wants. Next, check out the size of the company, to determine how much it will benefit from an increase in sales. A smaller company's earnings will improve from a hot selling product, whereas a larger company may not.

No. 9   Don't panic when a company or an industry becomes the target of the news media. If something unfavorable happened to the company (or industry), find out if it has enough financial strength (cash) to take it through economically hard times.

No. 10 Most investors put their money in the market too soon. Be patient. A potential winner might take one month or five years before it shows up. Then again, the Dow could drop 60% in a severe recession, or interest rates may climb to 18%. *Remember, the best opportunities always occur in the midst of a panic or a crisis.*

No. 11 *Wait until the entire industry experiences a crisis, then invest.* For example: banking, retailing, automotive, insurance companies, paper companies, technology companies, building suppliers, consumer products, etc. Because each of these industries are essential to the smooth operation of the economy, they will not disappear from the face of the earth in a severe recession or depression.

No. 12 Before you invest in an isolated industry or a foreign market, see if its products represent the future growth of the world's economy. For example, the Japanese now control 95% of all the electronic products in the United States. They realize it represents the 21st century and beyond.

No. 13 Multi-national corporations like MacDonald's and others should be purchased when interest rates are high. Lower interest rates will cause the dollar to fall, and this will translate into higher stock prices for the company doing business in a foreign land.

The Small Stock Effect

Small capitalization stocks have been severely undervalued since 1983. So keep a sharp eye out for further weaknesses in these markets. If the Dow severely crashes between 1992–2000 then small stocks could turn out to be the most profitable investment of the century.

A Simple Check List For New And Exciting Opportunities In The Business World

___ Does it make life simpler?

___ Is it unique?

___ Who has the patent on it?

___ Does the consumer love it?

___ Does it fulfill a basic human desire? (Smoking, drinking, entertainment, sex, the latest in affordable fashion.)

___ Does everyone recommend it, or talk about it?

___ Do you see people using it all the time, and they can't live without it?

___ If one person doesn't like it, that doesn't mean that the product or service is bad. Dig deeper. Chances are the person might have had some unusual experience with the product or service.

___ Does everyone shop or eat there?

___ Does is offer great services at affordable prices?

___ Does it have a loyal following?

___ How about the competition, what do they think of their competitors?

___ Is it something you must use every single day? One of life's necessities?

___ Has it sales grown dramatically, and only a few institutions own it?

___ Is it cool or fashionable to the teenager? (Like the "Gap" retail store.)

___ Is it profitable during a recession, like a deep discount retailer?

___ Does the company hold an exclusive patent on the product or drug?

___ Can it compete with larger companies?

___ Does it have a geographical niche? Is its location free from competitors?

___ Is anyone else making it, and if they are, how long will it take them to start production?

___ Is it addictive (food, alcohol, tobacco, pop)?

___ Does it fulfill a strong trend, such as jogging, physical fitness, aerobics, or skiing?

___ Will the government support it? That's a *big* plus. Does it have a lucrative government contract?

___ Are sales in foreign markets on the rise? Companies that can take advantage of foreign markets have an extra advantage over companies that cannot.

___ Is it a new wonder drug for a disabling disease? Will the consumer have to continue using the drug on a regular basis?

___ Can it improve business output? Is it a user of technology? (Many businesses will directly benefit from advances in technology as prices continue to fall.)

___ Does it have politically far-reaching effects? In other words, will the new administration endorse a policy that will benefit certain types of businesses (domestic or foreign)? For example, the Reagan administration encouraged stock takeovers and a strong national defense.

___ Look for new developments or changes taking place in the financial markets. For Example: During the 1970's the oil sector of the economy went through the roof when OPEC raised prices. Then in 1985 the collapse of OPEC helped propel the stock market to new all time highs. (Lower oil prices are anti-inflationary.)

____ Is it something the consumer will have to eventually protect themselves from? For example: rock music. It has been reported that more people will need hearing aids in the future. Plus, as we approach the year 2000, a growing number of senior citizens will require bifocals, as a large part of our society enter their golden years.

• Pollution control and waste management will become major problems in the future as the population continues to grow. Small aggressive companies in this area should experience the greatest growth. (Don't overlook heavy industrialized foreign markets.)

• Senior citizens will require treatment from bad backs or knees.

• Hospitals will require more beds as people grow older.

• More caskets and crematoriums will be needed, *especially* if there's a war.

• Telephone companies in Spain, Italy, and Mexico have been experiencing the greatest growth. What about a Russian telephone company? Think of how many business people will be calling each other in Russia as economic conditions gradually improve.

• Italy has one of the highest savings rates in the world. Look for its economy to continue to improve in the future.

• Lower priced fuel is great for airlines, the motel business, and popular vacation sights (like Disney).

• Which software programs are listed as best-sellers in popular computer magazines? Find out what the users think of these programs.

• Which retail stores are packed with enthusiastic shoppers? (Like Wal-Mart or Liz Claiborne.)

• The United States has the highest incidents of heart attack victims in the world. Check out the companies that make heart warning devices for someone that has recently had a heart attack (like Lifeline Inc.).

• New snack foods everyone enjoys. (Chewing gum fads.)

• Soda pop companies that have just gone public. Like Faygo and Shasta, owned by the National Beverage Company, in Fort Lauderdale, Fla.

• Low-price brand cigarette manufacturers in a recession, especially if tobacco taxes continue to rise.

• Look at all the computer or scientific magazines with the latest devices. Do any of them make any sense to the average consumer? Are they practical and affordable? Who makes them?

• Here's an intriguing idea: A research company just came out with a plastic that's ten times harder that steel. Imagine all the applications that could benefit from this breakthrough. They're also working on plastics that are 100 times harder than steel. Keep an eye out for new and exciting changes in this industry.

More Investment Ideas
For The 1990's

- Remember, the less Wall Street cares about a stock, the greater its profit potential when it finally catches on.

- The more the consumer relates to a new product or idea, the better its chance are of succeeding.

- Has the company recently reported an unexpected rise in sales or earnings?

- Does it have a large cash position? (Typically known as a "cash cow.") How many institutions own it? The fewer the better.

- Does the company have big write-offs it can use to temporarily offset its debts? Or hidden undervalued assets, like real estate?

- Do they avoid acquisitions into non-profitable ventures? (Are they buying every company in sight, simply because they don't know what to do with all the extra cash?)

- Research and development are crucial factors in maintaining the leading edge for many competitive industries. Drug companies, software developers, automotive advancements, chemical research. Find out how much they're spending, and on what.

- When you buy the stock of a big company or stalwart, wait until the market as a whole declines. Why? These companies are often the first to snap back when the market recovers. Buy a stalwart like Pepsi, Exxon, Phillip Morris, or Proctor & Gamble when something causes the price to fall dramatically. For example, a short time ago, Exxon was involved in a major lawsuit because of the famous Alaskan oil spill incident. Then, after a few years, the company's stock fully recovered.

- Always think about the future of a stock and the industry it occupies before making a long term investment.

- Stay away from industries that are capital intensive. (In other words companies that must re-invest a great deal of their profits back into the business, instead of using those profits to increase earnings.)

- Is the company developing a solid niche like Gannet did during the 1970's? This national distributor went around buying up every newspaper company in a single newspaper town, enabling the company to maintain exclusive territorial control of its products.

- Is the management, the board of directors, or are the employees buying back their own stock? (Insider buying.)

- Consider the market's PE ratio when it's high. Future economic projections rarely justify high PE's.

- When the stock market has been rising for some time, stay away from stocks, since the next bear market is rarely two to three years away.

• Be on the lookout for a severely depressed industry or a foreign market that is priced far below its intrinsic market value.

Be patient. Wait until the entire stock market crashes before you invest. Then go through this simple checklist:

____Has the company lowered its debt?

____How strong have the earnings been lately?

____How much cash do they have on hand?

____What kind of expansion plans do they have?

____Can they efficiently break into foreign markets with their products?

____How are the foreign market responding to these products?

____Are there any *political* changes that favor certain businesses and exclude others?

____Is the company buying back its own stock, and why? What is it doing that attracts insider attention?

____Can it still keep up with the competition?

____What kind of debt do they carry on their books? Bank debt is not favorable, since a bank can call in a loan at the first sign of trouble. Then there's funded debt; this kind of debt is ideal since it doesn't have to be repaid for the next fifteen to thirty years.

Special Situations To Watch For

• *Small companies generating large amounts of cash, or high returns on equity may have a unique product or service that deserves immediate attention.*

• *Spin-offs of large powerful companies have the best chance of succeeding, because the parent company assists the smaller company while its growing.*

• *Keep up with the company's financial history and any new developments taking place.*

• *Make sure that they're still coming out with good ideas that appeal to the consumer.*

• *Always buy a stock when it's at the lowest point in a cyclical industry. Examples are automotive, insurance, housing, building, mining, paper, aluminum, etc.*

• *Buy the stock of a company no one wants to own. Examples are companies involved in trash disposal, coffin manufacturing or mortuaries, toxic wastes, greasy solvents, automotive gukk, gambling casinos, or tobacco companies.*

• *Companies branching off into foreign markets can continue to grow as long as their products or services are effectively marketed.*

Has It Come Out With A New Consumer Related Patent?

The following is a list of the most profitable ideas of this century:

Air-Conditioners	Shopping Malls
Black & White TV	Smoke Detectors
Color TV	Fast Food Restaurants
Automatic Transmissions	Supermarkets
Magnetic Tape (Tape Recorders)	Transistors
LP Records	Micro-chips
Hi-Fi Equipment	Transparent Tape
Compact Discs	Frozen Foods
VCR (Video Rentals)	Health Insurance
The Pill	Latex Paints
Tampons	Paperback Books
Refrigerators, Freezers	Disposable Diapers
Washers and Dryers	Power Mowers
Detergents	Enriched Bread
Synthetic Fabrics	Credit Cards
The Polio Vaccine	Antibiotics
Personal Computers	Air Travel
Safety Belts	Industrialization
Running Shoes	Air-bags

(*and to clean up this mess* —Trash Removal!)

Remember, all you need are a few good investment ideas in a lifetime to come out on top. Then again, a few bad speculative moves could wipe out your entire financial future. Use common sense, don't speculate!

Does Anyone Really Know What They're Doing In The Stock Market?

Of course not. It's a gamble even if you're a genius.
(However, if you're a financial genius, it then becomes an intelligent gamble.)

Investors often assume that the average person knows what he or she is doing in the stock market. Unfortunately, there is no truth to this statement whatsoever. Most investors failed to make a profit during the biggest stock market advances of this century. Why? Because they either bought and sold their investments at the wrong time, or sold out at the very bottom of the crash.

• **What about financial institutions or mutual funds?**

Again, studies from the 1960's show that monkeys throwing darts at the stock section of a newspaper can easily outperform 95% of Wall Street's highest paid investment advisors.

Develop a way to think for yourself; don't let brokers or security analysts do it for you. You'll never get rich that way.

Why Invest In Japan?
Here's the best reason in the world: They're not about to build fifty thousand nuclear bombs like the United States and Russia did.

No. 1   Japan's Nekkia Index has grown 17-fold during the last 20 years, while the Dow Jones Industrial Averages has merely doubled.

No. 2   Japan owns 95% of all consumer related electronics in the United States, and the biggest auto industry in the world.

No. 3   Literacy in Japan approaches 100% (in the U.S. one out of four people cannot read or write). Japan also leads in the field of mathematics.

No. 4   Japan has the highest savings rate of any country in the world. Their household savings rate is approximately 14% per family as compared with 7% in the United States. Japan's personal financial assets exceed $6 trillion, whereas the United States has the lowest saving rate in the world, and the highest capital gains taxes.

No. 5   The Japanese economy is now the second largest in the world with a GNP of over $2.8 trillion. Japan's GNP per capita amounts to $24,382 (in U.S. dollars) placing it well ahead of the U.S. ($19,819), Germany ($19,124), and Canada ($18,273).

No. 6   Japan has over 2,600 publicly traded companies.

No. 7   The Japanese culture, life-style, and work ethic contribute to corporate performance.

No. 8   Japan's government supports corporate profitability, and their corporate tax rates are extremely low, whereas the United States has the highest corporate tax rates in the world.

No. 9   The price earnings ratios are higher in Japan than in the United States. Why? Our federal deficit constantly inhibits growth by sending interest rates higher, thereby strangling corporate profitability.

Special Alert To Foreign Investors: The Japan Fund
The Nekkia Index has lost 40% to 50% from its all time high. (As of 1992)

Many of the world's best investors have bought into the Japan fund, and will continue to buy more as it falls. The growth of this fund has been phenomenal since the early 1960's. $10,000 invested in 1960 is worth an astonishing $1,383,891 today! Phone No. 1-800-53-JAPAN.

How To Spot A Market High

- When the PE ratio of the S&P 500 is over 18, and the Dows PE is between 20 and 30.

- When the dividend yields on stocks are under 3%.

- When the odd lotters come back into the market, on larger amounts of volume.

- If interest rates are at their lowest levels for the past five to ten years.

- The Federal Reserve may raise its reserve requirements to banks, causing interest rates to rise.

- Stock market volume has days when it sets record-breaking highs.

- Option speculation is going through the roof.

- Ask a broker if he's been getting a flood of new-issue buyers lately. The Investor's Daily newspaper has a special section devoted to this kind of information.

- Margin requirements on stocks are sometimes tightened in order to eliminate excess speculation in the market.

- At the end of a bull market in stocks, gold prices rise because the economy starts overheating. (Stronger growth may lead to inflationary pressures.)

- Most financial experts have turned into super bulls. Look for the percentage of financial advisors that are bullish; the higher the percentage rate the greater the danger. The Wall Street Journal or Barron's market laboratory has a special section devoted to this kind of information.

- Prices for a seat on the major financial exchanges have risen to astronomical levels.

- Magazine articles are packed with stories about outstanding mutual fund managers.

- Aggressive mutual funds are at the top of the list when it comes to investment returns. And many of them have made unusually large percentage gains in a short period of time.

- You receive dozens of investment newsletters from financial advisors all claiming to have developed a stock market system that will generate five million dollars in profits in less than five minutes.

- Brokers you haven't heard from in five or ten years call you up to inform you that this is the greatest bull market of all time. (This always happens at the end of a super bull market.)

- Financial advisors inconveniently call you up at 8 or 9 o'clock in the evening with the greatest stock picks of the century.

- A growing number of financial advisors become god-like heroes in the public's eye. (The type that peddle wave theories and other useless schemes.)

- Investors start bragging about their huge gains, and many investors think that they're going to get rich in a short period of time.
- Financial magazines like *Barron's, The Wall Street Journal,* and others, are loaded with the mug shots of every financial guru in town, all claiming to have made incredible profits in a short period of time.

How To Spot A Market Low

- Dividend yields on stocks are well over 3%.
- The PE ratio for the S&P 500 is 12 or less.
- Interest rates are above the stock markets historical highs (9%), while thirty-year treasury bonds are hitting new lows.
- The Federal Reserve drops its discount rate two times in succession, 1/2-percent each time. Or it may drop interest rates one full percentage point to stimulate the economy.
- Pessimism is everywhere, because no one wants to put the first dollar in the market. *Stock market volume has reached record lows.*
- People start referring to the current economic crisis as if it were the next Great Depression.
- An unusual number of business bankruptcies, plant shutdowns, or layoffs have occurred.
- A large sell-off usually takes place as the Dow makes it's final plunge. *Volume may exceed several hundred million shares a day in the final sell-off.*
- Most financial analysts are extremely bearish even though prices have never been lower.
- Your stock broker has loads of free time to talk to you since no one wants to invest in the market.
- Most newsletters continually urge the investor to stay on the sidelines. (Of course, this usually turns out to be the best time to buy!)
- The Federal Reserve may loosen the requirements on stock market margin at the very bottom of a severe bear market crash. The Fed will also lower interest rates or raise the level of cash available to reserve banks. *The Wall Street Journal* or *Barron's* market laboratory has a special section devoted to this kind of information.
- Check the percentage of financial advisors that are bearish. The higher the percentage, the greater the chances of a market recovery. Again, *The Wall Street Journal* or *Barron's* market laboratory has a special section devoted to this kind of information.

Last Remarks: Follow the investment strategies in Chapter IV or V, and use the information on pages 37-38 to assist you when the market rises or falls. Pay special attention to interest rate movements, since they have a powerful effect on the economy.

Chapter IV
Income and Bond Strategies

Do You Get Your Thrills From T-Bills?

The Federal deficit is expected to reach $5 trillion in 1995.

At this alarming rate of growth a credit crisis could easily send interest rates soaring to post—1980 levels. When this happens, purchase long-term U.S. treasury bonds or high grade corporate bonds during a credit crisis.[1] (i.e., since the long-term historical average for stocks has been 9%, make sure that the prevailing interest rates are 10% or higher at 1991 levels.)[2]

If you're worried about inflation (and who isn't), use the gold system in Chapter V to protect your portfolio from an unprecedented rise from inflation.

How To Trade Zero's, Long Term T-Bonds, Or Bond Mutual Funds During A Credit Crisis

Use a thirty-year government zero bond, or a bond mutual fund that primarily invests in long-term zeros or thirty-year treasury notes. Investors in a higher tax bracket should consider long-term municipal bonds.

Follow the directions below:

No. 1   If interest rates are low, keep your money in a short-term money market fund, *with a low expense fee.*

No. 2   When interest rates start to rise, the Federal government will raise the discount rate to its lending banks. This will signal the banks to raise their prime lending rate one-half of a percentage point to one full percentage point each time.

No. 3   As interest rates continue to rise above 10% or more, keep following them until they've peaked. (At that point the Dow may have lost 20%–30% from its former high.[3]) Once interest rates have peaked, the Federal Reserve will start to cut interest rates.

For Example:

Let's say that interest rates have been rising for a year and a half, and the prevailing rate is 13% for long-term bonds. If the Federal Reserve board cuts interest rates two times in succession (1/2 of a percentage point each time, or one full percent), *invest your capital at this point.*

No. 4   Follow the gold system in Chapter V to protect your bond portfolio against inflation. (If inflation accelerates, the gold system will temporary offset any losses that you may have acquired during this period.)

---

[1]Investors in higher tax brackets may consider municipal bonds instead.
[2]By following the special instructions in this chapter.
[3]The lower the Dow falls the higher the return will be on interest rates, especially during a credit crisis.

Bond Or Bond Mutual Fund Owners:

No. 1   Take your profits as bond prices appreciate or interest rates fall in
price. For example, if interest rates drop on a bond purchased at 12%
to 11%, skim off the profits and put them back in your money market
fund. Consequently, if interest rates start rising again to 13%, 14%, or
15%, invest the profits from the money market fund *into* a long-term
bond *or* bond fund.

No. 2   Assuming that you're using the Gold System in Chapter V, remember
to take 20% of the profits that you make from the bond fund, and place
them into the Gold system's money market fund. For example: If you
received $1000 in profit from your bond fund, switch $200 or 20%
into the gold money market account, and adjust it according to the
instructions in the Gold System. (Please refer to the Gold System in
Chapter V for more details on this procedure.)

Special Note:

*Mutual fund managers often lessen interest rate risk by purchasing
bonds with different outstanding maturities. If you want the highest
interest rate available, buy the bonds directly from a bank or the
Treasury.*

Is The Stock Market Dead In The United States?
What can an investor do, short of revolution?

In the following example, we will examine the return from a bond fund
using the strategies in this chapter.[2]

Year 1	8%	Year 6	8%
Year 2	7%	Year 7	8%
Year 3	6%	Year 8	7%
Year 4	7%	Year 9	15%
Year 5	30%	Year 10	6%

A $10,000 investment grew into $26,000 or 10% compounded.

Keep your money in a good paying money market fund until the bond
market crashes (a period associated with high interest rates). Then slowly
switch back from a long-term bond fund into a money market fund as interest
rates decline. Follow the strategy on the top of page 43, in order to substantially
increase the return from your income investments.

---

[1]In one year.
[2]Between the 1980's and 1990's, money markets earned 12.8% compounded annually.

If the investor switches from a bond fund to a stock fund during a severe stock market crash,[1] and the mutual fund makes 50% during the eleventh year, the compounded rate of growth will have increased from 10% to 13.8%. Since the long term averages for the stock market have been around 9% to 10%, this method of investment has dramatically increased the total return of the portfolio by nearly three percentage points. From then on the income investor should use the modified version of the Aggressive Mutual Fund System below, or the Aggressive Mutual Fund System in Chapter V in order to keep his/her compounded rate of growth at the 13.8% level.

Modified Version Of The Aggressive Mutual Fund System

After the investor places his/her money in a severe stock market crash, he/she may follow the investment strategy below, or use the *Aggressive Mutual Fund System* in Chapter V.

No. 1   First, place 20% of your portfolio's total value in the Gold System. See Chapter V.

No. 2   Take your profits from the stock fund 10% at a time as the market recovers.

No. 3   Invest 50% of these profits when the Dow crashes -17% or more from its previous all time high.[2] Then invest the remainder in a stock fund when the Dow falls 35% or more from its all time high. (Follow the Gold System carefully, then if the economy slips into a depression, use the directions in Chapter 6 titled, "How to Invest in a Depression.")

No. 4   Any new monies that the income investor acquires should be placed in a separate account until the stock market severely crashes again.

In addition to the above strategies, please follow the special investment techniques that are located on pages 71-73.

The Profit Potential Of Government Guaranteed Zero Bonds With The Longest Maturity

The table on the following page shows the adjusted compounded return for a 30-year treasury zero bond taxed at 30%. Inflation has been figured in at 5% for 30 years. (The figures below were calculated after taxes and inflation have been deducted.)

The stock market's average for the last 120 years has been 9% a year. These figures are somewhat lower if the losses are deducted from mutual fund expense fees, taxes, and inflation.

---

[1] In one year.
[2] When the Dow has lost 35% or more from its all time high, and small cap mutual funds have lost 55% to 70% of their value.

The Adjusted Return From A 30-Year Government Zero Bond *After* Taxes And Inflation Have Been Deducted

Adjusted for an annual inflation rate of 5%.

12% $299,599
       (Total return after inflation 5.1 times your original investment.)

13% $437,498
       Total return after inflation 9.7 times your original investment.)

14% $579,464
       Total return after inflation 12.8 times your original investment.)

15% $766,492
       Total return after inflation 17 times your original investment.)

16% $1,025,695
       Total return after inflation 22.7 times your original investment.)

Remember that zeros pay no interest until maturity, and you must pay Federal taxes each year on the accrued interest, whereas T-Bonds pay out simple interest two times a year, *lowering* the effective yield of the bond.

The One Minor Problem With Zero's

The government could exercise a call on the bond within five years from the date of its maturity.

The figures below have been adjusted for a 30-year zero bond called in at 25 years *after* taxes and inflation were deducted. (Figuring 5% annually for inflation.)

13% $328,753
       (Total return after inflation 7.6 times your original investment.)

14% $415,629
       (Total return after inflation 9.6 times your original investment.)

15% $524,582
       (Total return after inflation 12.1 times your original investment.)

16% $833,642
       (Total return after inflation 15.3 times your original investment.)

Why Bonds?

1. During a credit crisis, bonds are perhaps the safest most profitable investments imaginable, since there are no management fees to pay, unlike mutual funds.

2. Government long-term bonds have no early call provisions to worry about, unlike corporate bonds.

Chapter V
The Master's Greatest Strategies

Welcome To The Greatest Investment Strategies Of The Twentieth Century

100 Years, from 1892-1992
There were sixty-six great ten-year holding periods when small stocks on average achieved 20% compounded returns.

In order to achieve the above return, the investor had to purchase stocks in the depths of a terrible bear market, when the Dow lost 39% to 89% of its value.[1] The *lowest* returns for each of these sixty-six ten-year holding periods resulted in a meager 0.8% gain. This occurred as investors were purchasing stocks near the market's high.

100 Years, from 1892-1992
There were forty-five holding periods when small stocks on average achieved a 14.5% compounded return.[1]

In order to achieve the above return, the investor had to purchase stocks in the depths of a terrible bear market, when the Dow lost 39% to 89% of its value. The *lowest* returns for each of these forty-five holding periods resulted in a 5.9% gain. This occurred as investors were purchasing stocks near the market's high. *The reader may now be saying,* "I'll just invest my money in the stock market when it takes a severe beating, and hope for the best . . ."

However:

- Can you identify those rare times when small capitalization stocks or mutual funds lost 60% to 70% of their value?[2] (Like 1969–70, or 1973–74.)

- Are you patient enough to wait at least ten years for the stock market to drop to these levels?

- Can you accumulate enough wealth in the meantime to make such an investment worthwhile?

1929 – Dow lost 90%
1937 – Dow lost 49%
1940 – Dow lost 39%
1969 – Dow lost 36%
1973 – Dow lost 45%
1987 – Dow lost 37%

Many small stock funds lost 60%–95% of their value during these periods.

---

[1]This assumes that the investor was lucky enough to sell out near the highs of the markets price range during each of these 10-year intervals.
[2]The investor may hear financial news reports saying that this is the worst market crash of the last 10 or 20 years. This will tip you off that it's the perfect time to invest in the hardest hit industries, sector funds, or small cap mutual funds.

How To Make Big Money
In The Stock Market

Wait until the stock market totally collapses.
(At the Federal deficits current rate of growth disaster is just around the corner!)

From 1975 to 1991, many of the top performing small cap mutual funds returned 2000%–3000%. However, this meant that the investor had to do most of his/her buying near the market lows in 1975, after these funds lost 60% to 70% of their value.[1]

In order to achieve the same investment results as those obtained above, wait until the Dow falls at least 35% or more from its high,[2] and then purchase outstanding small stock mutual funds that have dropped 60% to 70% in value.

For a list of the mutual funds that achieved the best long-term investment results from the 1973–1974 crash, see Chapter II, "Mutual Funds and Reality," under the heading, The World's Greatest Investors Top Choices for the 1990's and Beyond.

Will Gold Mutual Funds Protect You
During An Economic Crisis?
Only if you use the investment strategies in this chapter!

Financial advisors often recommend avoiding gold because of its extreme volatility. However:

No. 1   During the 1920's, stocks were making enormous returns. Then, in the 1930's the stock market severely crashed, erasing all of the former gains of the previous decade. Gold stocks were the only sector of the economy that made astonishing returns of 500% or more (see the Homestake Mining Tables at the back of this book).

No. 2   When the inflationary policies of the 1970's shattered the stock market and much of the economy, gold mining stocks once again soared to record breaking levels. (According to Solomon Brothers, gold achieved a 31.9% compounded return between 1970–1980.) *Unfortunately, most investors failed to make a profit because of the gold markets extreme volatility.*

No. 3   If the Federal government ever defaults on its debt obligations, gold mining stocks could easily repeat the fabulous returns they made during the 1930's and 1970's. Assuming that such an event were to take place in the 1990's, investors could easily make another fortune by taking their gold profits and purchasing stocks on a newly formed stock exchange. (Prices on the major exchanges could drop to the lowest levels ever recorded!)

---

[1]Again, this assumes that the investor was lucky enough to sell out near the highs.
[2]Or a strong foreign economy that has lost 35% or more of its value in a crash.

Question: Are gold mutual funds or stocks worth owning during an economic crash?

Answer: Yes. Just remember to use the special gold trading system in this chapter.

Correlation Between Stock, Bond, Or Gold Prices
Source: Solomon Brothers

Between 1970–1980, the investments below returned the following compounded gains:

Gold	31.8%	$10,000 grew into $160,000[1]
Oil	24%	
Stocks	8.7%	$10,000 grew into $22,000
T-bills	7.7%	
Bonds	6.6	
Inflation Index	7.8% [2]	

Correlation Between Stock, Bond, Or Gold Prices
Part II
Source: Solomon Brothers.

Between 1980–1990, the investments below returned the following compounded gains:

Stocks	16.5%	$10,000 grew into $46,000
Bonds	12.8%	$10,000 grew into $33,000
T-bills	9.8%	
Gold	2.5%	
Inflation Index	4.6% [3]	

During the 1970's, Gold was King of the financial markets with a 31.6% compounded return.[1] Then in the 1980's, common stocks achieved the highest return for the decade.

The Reverse Compounding Chart

The reverse compounding chart on page 84 will help the investor understand the beneficial effects of compounding in a bear market. Study the profit potential of an investment when it falls 50%, 60%, or 70% in value.

For example: If an investment makes 100% and then loses 50% of its value, the entire 100% profit will have been erased from the 50% loss.

However: If the investor buys into a fund that lost 50%, *it will make 100% when it fully recovers.* Why? Because it will have to rise 100% to break even.

---

[1]This figure assumes that the investor bought in at the lows and sold at the highs.
[2]$10,000 required $20,000 just to break even with inflation; figure does not include taxes for the period.
[3]$10,000 required $15,000 just to break even with inflation; figure does not include taxes.

A Good Example Of Reverse Compounding

Examine the Homestake Mining tables from 1929–1936 in the back of this book, and compare them with the Dow's Jones Industrial averages for the same period.[1] Take a careful look at the price spread between gold stocks and the falling Dow. Then figure out how much you could have made by periodically taking your gold profits and re-investing them in a stock market crash.[2] (Use the reverse compounding chart as a guide.) This is a wonderful exercise in what I call reverse compounding, and I hope the reader understands the importance of learning this extremely valuable mathematical formula.

Investors: Relax, Be Patient; You're Not Going To Die

And if you are, it's too late anyway.

Pep Talk Time

The stock market for 1992 and beyond will continue to be a bargain hunter's dream, as long as you remain confident in the bumbling nature of our political system. On one hand, there's always the possibility of long-term interest rates climbing above 12% in a deep recession. On the other hand, gold stocks could easily set new highs during an economic crisis. Anything is possible. Troubled times spell great opportunities for the patient investor, and patience is perhaps the greatest gift we human beings possess.[3]

Question: Are The Strategies In This Chapter Similar To Asset Allocation?

No, the strategies in this chapter are far more flexible than asset allocation. Asset allocation tries to forecast future economic events by assigning a certain amount of capital to different sectors of the economy. In comparison, the investment techniques in this chapter will automatically react to the future by adapting to the changes that occur in the market place while there unfolding.

If "Modern Portfolio Theory" Is Such A Great Idea, Then Why Does It Just Sit There And Do Nothing?

Modern Portfolio Theory (MPT) is often better in principal than in practice. The theory suggests that the practitioner spread 25% to 35% of his/her investment capital between stocks, bonds, and gold. Then apparently each investment will compensate for the other's losses during an economic crisis.

---

[1] All figures are located in the same table.
[2] The trouble is that most of the profits in the gold market quickly disappeared because of its extreme volatility. The trading system in this chapter was designed to correct this problem by taking profits and reinvesting them during a stock market crash.
[3] Unfortunately we were raised in a very impatient society, so this make patience an even *greater* virtue.

Unfortunately, the biggest gap in this theory comes from the fact that MPT fails to maximize the profits from each of these areas of the economy efficiently. Ironically, MPT just sits there while your profits disappear. (Which is exactly what happened in the volatile gold markets of the 1970's.) The strategies in this chapter will dramatically improve the missing function of MPT by re-positioning profits from the strongest sector of the economy to the weakest. For example, if the investor captured the growing profits from a typical gold mutual fund during the 1970's, and placed them in the next weakest sector of the economy (like a stock market crash), or the bond crash of 1981–84, then the investor could take full advantage of the weakest and strongest sectors of the economy more efficiently, and thereby accumulate greater compounded returns from his/her investments.

The Incredible Gold Trading System

How to accumulate greater profits from your gold mutual fund, and protect your stock or bond mutual fund from the adverse effects of inflation or deflation.

Historically speaking, the gold market can be extremely volatile during an economic crisis. For example, between 1970 and 1980, the average investor could have accumulated 1600% in profits from an investment in gold. Unfortunately, most of these profits disappeared in two of the biggest gold market crashes of this century. (The Gold System was designed to take the growing profits from a gold fund and re-invest them when prices have dropped significantly.)

Important Note: Avoid gold mutual funds that add gold bullion to their portfolios. This system requires extreme volatility in order to capture most of the profits from a rising gold market. (Refer to the Homestake Mining tables at the end of this book.)

Important Note: Later on in this chapter we'll show you how to couple the gold trading system with the aggressive mutual fund system for maximum profit potential.

PART I (Of The Gold System).

Follow the directions below:

• Set up a money market fund (name it *Money Market No. 2*).

• Take 20% of your portfolio's total value and invest it in a gold mutual fund or a closed-end fund.

> To start, place 20% of the portfolio's total value in *Money Market No. 2* and then divide it up into bi-monthly investments. For example, let's say that your total portfolio's value is $10,000. (Twenty percent of this amount is $2,000.)
>
> *Formulae:* $10,000 x 20% = $2,000
>
> Divide this amount up 6 times a year, or bi-monthly. Then invest $160 every other month in a gold fund.

Formulae: $160 divided by the previous figure
represents 8% of $2,000, or ($2,000 x 8% = $160)

*Later on when additional capital is added to the gold money market fund,
readjust the account according to the directions below.*

- $160 is being invested bi-monthly according to the above plan. Then $2,500 is received (from your place of employment; a bonus, perhaps).

  First, invest the $2500 by placing $500 or 20%, in the gold money market fund, and $2000 or 80%, in the aggressive mutual fund system (see Pages. 52–57),

- Readjust your bi-monthly investment plan as follows:

  $2,500 x 8% = $200

  At this point the investor should add $200 from the gold money market fund to a gold mutual fund, on a bi-monthly basis.

One More Example:

The investor recently acquires $5,000.

First, invest $1,000, or 20%, in the gold money market fund system, and 80%, or $4000, in the aggressive mutual fund system (see Pages. 52–57.)

At this point the gold money market account will be worth approximately $3,500 *because $2500 was previously invested.*

$3,500 x 8% = $280

From then on the investor should add $280 from the gold money market fund to the gold mutual fund, on a bi-monthly basis.

Please Note: Always figure the *highest* dollar amount in the gold fund as the figure to multiply by 8%. If the value of the account falls, ignore it; just continue with the plan until all the money has been invested.

Aggressive Mutual Fund Investors
Read Carefully

When you make a 10% profit from the aggressive mutual fund system (on Pages 52–57), place 20% of the stock fund's profit *directly* into the gold money market. (Then adjust it according to the above example.)

If you recently acquired $2000 in profits from your *stock mutual fund*, invest $400 (or 20%) of this directly into the gold money market account. (I.e., make sure that the gold system is adjusted for the additional capital.)

For Example: Let's say that you started with ($2,000) in the gold money market fund, and your bi-monthly investments have been $2,000 x 8% = $160.

Suddenly the gold money market is worth $2,400. Why?

Because 20% (or $400) was added in from the aggressive mutual fund's profits to the gold money market fund. Again, follow the same procedure as before:

$$\$2,400 \times 8\% = \$192.$$

At this point the investor should add $192 from the gold money market fund to the gold mutual fund, bi-monthly.

For the Aggressive Mutual Fund Investor Only

Again, what do we mean by 20% of the stock market profits from the aggressive mutual fund system?

- Let's say that your *stock* mutual fund just made $1000 in profit.

  Take 20% of $1000 (or $200), and place it in the gold money market account. Then make sure that you re-adjust the gold money market in order to compensate for the additional capital.

PART II

Time For Profit Taking *(Take profits 20% at a time)*

Periodically check the total value of your gold mutual fund by adding up the original dollar amounts that were previously invested in the fund. For example, let's say that the *original investments* totaled $2,000, and the gold mutual fund is presently worth $2,400. This means that you made a 20% profit. Call your mutual fund representative, and switch $400 from the gold mutual fund back into the gold money market. (Again, re-adjust the gold money market account in order to compensate for the additional capital).

Special Instructions: When you take the profits from the gold fund (20% at a time), s*kip* the next bi-monthly investment. However, if the gold market takes a big dive that month, simply invest as you normally would.

This procedure will automatically take profits in a rising market, and re-invest them in a falling market. (When prices have dropped considerably.)

For Example:

Let's start with $2000:

$$\$2000 \times 8\% = \$160$$

Invest this amount bi-monthly.

Let's say that you received $1000 in stock or bond market profits. Take 20% of this, or $200, and place it in the gold money market fund.

- Then re-adjust your bi-monthly investment as follows:

$$\$2,200 \times 8\% = \$176$$

At this point you should add $176 from the gold money market fund to the gold mutual fund on a bi-monthly basis.

**Aggressive Mutual Fund System Users,
Or Bond And Income Investors**

The Gold System only requires 20% of the total value of the portfolio!

When the stock market has declined sharply (*i.e.,* the Dow or a strong foreign fund has lost 35% or more from its all time high), add up the combined value of the gold money market fund and the gold fund. If you find that the Gold System exceeds 20% of the total value of the portfolio, take the additional capital from the gold money market fund and invest it in your stock mutual fund when the Dow has crashed 17% or more from its all time high (or if interest rates are unusually high on long-term Treasury bonds).

How To Adjust The Gold System

• Whenever the gold market goes up in price (in other words when it isn't in a crash phase), always invest 4% in a gold mutual fund bi-monthly. If the gold market continues to accelerate at an abnormal rate of speed, reduce your bi-monthly investments from 4% to 3% or 2.5% instead. *This procedure will substantially reduce the risk of buying higher priced gold shares right before the market crashes.*

• If the gold market crashes (-30% to -50% from its high), instead of the usual 4%, invest 6% to 8% during this bi-monthly period.[1] *(Our investment newsletter always keeps track of this vital information.)*

• When there is a *severe* drop in the price of gold from its high (-50% to -70%), increase your bi-monthly investment to 10% or 12%. Finally, if the gold market loses 70% or more of its value, invest 20% bi-monthly.[1]

Special Instructions: Stock or bond investors: during a severe stock market crash, switch half of the proceeds from the gold system into the stock market, especially if gold prices have been rising dramatically.

Predictions, Predictions
Where For Art Thou, Useless Predictions?

Rather than rely on useless forecasts or predictions that always fail when you need them, this strategy removes most of the profits from the gold fund before the market peaks. *This way you will always have the profits working for you, not against you.* If you don't take your profits, all of the capital gains will eventually disappear in a crash, and it may take several years before the fund fully recovers.

How Does This Unique System Continually Adjust Itself
When New Profits Are Added?

---

[1] Continue to invest the recommended percentages bi-monthly as long the market stays or drops below these levels.

First, let's start out with the original investment:

we started with
$$\$2000 \times 8\% = \$160.$$
Invested bi-monthly for 6 months a year, this equals $960 a year.

The bi-monthly plan continued for a two year period,
$$\$960 \times 2 = \$1920$$
By the end of two years, $2,000 was invested.

Example: Let's say that the investor earns $500 from the gold fund at the end of the first year (because gold prices went up). Since $960 was previously invested in the gold fund, a total of $1040 remains to be invested. At that point an additional $500 profit was switched into the gold money market fund, raising its value from $1040 to $1540. Since this amount was lower than the $2,000 previously invested, we continue to figure the *highest* amount originally invested in the fund which was $2000 x 8% = $160. The investor should continue adding the usual $160 every other month until the money market fund has been fully invested, or additional capital is added into the gold money market fund.

Why Does The Gold System Turn Over Its Portfolio On A Two Year Basis?

The price spread between stock market crashes and rising gold prices are most effective when they are spaced no further than two years apart.[1] The Homestake Mining Tables located at the end of this book will clearly point out the advantages of having a small percentage of your portfolio invested in gold mutual funds just before a severe stock market crash begins.

Why Is This Strategy So Remarkable?
Because it's extremely flexible.

This strategy continually pyramids investment capital between a money market fund and a gold mutual fund,[2] allowing the investor to pick up additional gold shares at lower price levels. It also safeguards profits as they build up, and reinvests them in a severe stock market crash.

Taking Profits 10% At A Time Before They Disappear

$10,000 at 100%, total $7,000 profit.

---

[1] Just in case a major crash occurs within a two year period, the majority of the money in the gold system will have already been invested.
[2] When interest rates rise, gold prices eventually fall.

Starting out with a $10 investment, profits are taken 10% at a time.

$10,000   Share price $10   to $11   we made $1,000
$10,000   Share price $11   to $12.1   we made another $1000
$10,000   Share price $12.1   to $13.31   we made another $1000
$10,000   Share price $13.31 to $14.64   we made another $1000
$10,000   Share price $14.64 to $16.10   we made another $1000
$10,000   Share price $16.10 to $17.71   we made another $1000
$10,000   Share price $17.71 to $19.48   we made another $1000

Total $17,000

This table will reveal the consequences of taking profits 10% at a time:

For a 10% profit the market must rise 10%
For a 20% profit the market must rise 21%
For a 30% profit the market must rise 33%
For a 40% profit the market must rise 46%
For a 50% profit the market must rise 61%
For a 60% profit the market must rise 75%
For a 70% profit the market must rise 95%

The Aggressive Mutual Fund Trading System

*A stock portfolio or closed-end fund may be
used instead of a mutual fund.*

The First Method:

An actual ten-year study is provided on pages 63–66 titled, "The Stock Market System." Study it *only* as a reference to this easy to use formula.

During the course of this chapter we will be referring to the Dow Jones Industrials highest high. Please read the following paragraph for a brief explanation of this phenomenon.

What Is The "Highest High"?

Let's say the Dow made it to the 3000 mark.
Then later on it reaches a new high of 3100.
Shortly after it reaches 3100, the
Dow drops to 2015, losing 35% of its value.

Use the following equation:

$$3100 \times 35\% = 1085$$

Then take 3100 - 1085 = 2015.

When the Dow falls to the 2015 level, invest in a small stock mutual fund.

Next Example: Let's say that the Dow climbs back to 3500, and falls to 2905:

3500 x 17% = 595 [then subtract]
3500 - 595 = 2905 (invest at 2905 or below.)

Final Example: Dow sets a new all-time high of 4000, then falls 680 points When this happens take your calculator and figure:

3500 x 17% = 595 [then subtract]
3500 - 595 = 2905 (invest at 2905 or below.)

Now For The System:

• Before you begin, place 20% of your total portfolio's value in the gold system (as explained in the previous chapter). This will protect the entire portfolio during a depressionary or inflationary crisis.

• Use the second or third method supplements, and the anti-climatic effect on pages 71–74.

• Follow the steps, below, the very first time you invest in a stock market crash, then use the section titled "When the Stock Market Crashes the Next Time," for any crash thereafter.

The First Step: Create Two Funds: A money market fund (call it *Money Market No. 1),* and an aggressive growth fund. (Make sure that the mutual fund doesn't use options, margin, or futures.)

When the Dow falls 17% or more from its all time high, take 40% of the entire portfolio's value from *Money Market Fund No. 1,* and invest it in a small stock growth fund.

When the Dow falls 35% or more from its all time high, take the *remainder* of the money from *Money Market No. 1, plus* the money from the Gold System and add it to the aggressive stock fund. *Just remember to leave 10% of your portfolio's total value in the gold mutual fund before the crash lowered its value. Use your previous financial statements as a guide.*

For Example: If the total value of the portfolio (before the market peaked) added up to $100,000, keep 10% of $100,000 or $10,000, in a gold mutual fund. If the stock market continues its downward trend and gold prices continue to rise, invest the profits from the gold fund directly into a stock mutual fund. This is explained in Chapter VI titled, "How To Invest in a Depression."

What About High Interest Rates On Bonds?
Good question!

If the Dow crashes 17% or more from its all time high and interest rates are still rising sharply, wait until the Fed starts lowering the discount rate by one percent. At that point, switch the capital from *Money Market No. 1* (the aggressive mutual fund money market), and *Money Market No. 2* (the gold fund money market), into a long term bond fund. Take your profits six to seven percent from the Dow's former high as interest rates decline. After this occurs take additional profits 10% at a time or sell the long-term bonds and place the proceeds back into the money market accounts.

Read Carefully

Check the amount of accrued interest received in *Money Market No. 1* from your monthly financial statements.[1] Then switch 20% of the accrued interest into *Money Market No. 2* (adjust the Gold System for the additional capital). *Just make sure that the statement shows the interest received on* Money Market No. 1 *only.*

For Example: Let's say that *Money Market No. 1* made $500 in interest during the past 6 months. Multiply:

$$\$500 \times 20\% = \$125$$

Switch this amount into the gold money market fund, and adjust that fund according to the directions in the Gold System.

How To Take Your Profits:

For an explanation on the following procedure, please refer to Chapter I under the heading, "The Dreaded Wall of Worry Syndrome."

Take profits 10% at a time; as the Dow approaches its previous all-time high.[2] Follow the anti-climatic strategies on pages 73–74.

The short-term benefits of long-term capital gains:

Instead of taking profits 10% at a time, investors could take profits along with long-term capital gains when the Dow approaches its previous all- time high. (Please time this event carefully; in other words, don't throw away a profit just because there's a tax break. A profit is still a profit).

The Reason For This Procedure

Question: Most stock market advisors instruct you to sell all your holdings when they think the market is high. Why do you leave some investment capital in?

Answer: Faced with the insurmountable difficulty of trying to time the markets highs and lows, the best solution is to take profits 10% at a time in order to protect these earnings from disappearing in a severe bear market crash. Later on when the market has risen to *sky high valuations* it might be wise to trim off another 5% or 10% from your stock market holdings at that time.

---

[1] By checking your financial statements from your mutual fund or brokerage every six months to a year.
[2] This procedure also includes long-term bonds. You should take any accumulated profit from a bond fund when the stock market is 6% to 7% from its former all-time high, especially if interest rates have been falling dramatically.

When The Stock Market Crashes
The Second Time

Follow these steps at the beginning of the second stock market crash:

- When the Dow falls 17% or more from its all-time high, add up the total amount of the portfolio, then add 40% of your portfolio's total value to a stock mutual fund.

- If you originally invested $10,000 in your stock fund and during a crash the value drops to $8,000, locate your old financial statements and find out how much the entire portfolio was worth before the crash. After you have figured out this amount invest the difference in a brand new stock fund. Use the following example as a reference.

- *Example:* Let's say that your stock fund is worth $10,000; then a crash lowers the Dow 17% or more. When this happens, add up the entire value of the portfolio and make sure 40% is invested in the stock fund. In other words, if the stock fund's value was $10,000 before the crash lowered stock prices, and it will presently take $14,000 to make the stock fund equal 40% of the portfolio's total value, add $4,000 to a *brand new stock fund*.[1] Later, when both mutual funds are making a profit from the original amounts invested, switch all of the money from the newly acquired stock mutual fund back into the original fund, and continue taking profits 10% at a time.

For a somewhat clearer example of this technique, please read the paragraph titled, "The Profit Potential and Safety of the Aggressive Mutual Fund System," *in Chapter V. (See Years Four and Seven, first paragraph.)*

If the investor would rather use stocks or closed-end funds instead of mutual funds, then set up two separate accounts at a deep discount brokerage, and follow the same procedure as above. See the section in this chapter titled, "The Cheapest Brokerages in America."

When the Dow falls 35% or more from its all time high, take all the money from your entire portfolio except 10% of the gold fund, and invest it in the stock market.[2] In addition, when the Dow falls below 35% or more from its high, follow the special Gold Depression System on the next page.

Attention: Real Estate Owners

Extremely sophisticated investors may borrow additional capital for the purchase of mutual funds or sector funds during a crash. Please follow the advice in this chapter titled, "How To Use Real Estate to Pyramid Your Way to Wealth in the Stock or Bond Markets."

---

[1]Or the same mutual fund with a different account number.
[2]Figure 10% of your entire portfolio's value when it was at its highest total dollar value right before the market crashed. For example, if the total value of the portfolio at the highest point before the crash was $100,000 then keep 10% of $100,000 which is $10,000, in the gold mutual fund. (Use your statements as a reference.)

Read Carefully

Check the accrued interest received in *Money Market No. 1* from your monthly statements.[1] Then switch 20% of this amount into *Money Market No. 2* (remember to adjust the Gold System). Just make sure that the statement shows the interest received on *Money Market No. 1* only.

• *For Example:* Let's say that *Money Market No. 1* made $500 in interest during the past 6 months.

Multiply: $500 x 20% = $125

• Switch the above amount from *Money Market No. 1* into *Money Market No. 2*, and adjust *Money Market No. 2* according to the directions in the Gold System.

The Gold Depression System

Special Directions For A Depression Or An Economic Crisis:

When the Dow Jones Industrial Averages falls 35% or more, make sure that you leave at least 10% of your portfolio's total value in a gold mutual fund (just in case the economy ends up in a depression). For example, let's say that the stock market (Dow) has recently been through a severe crash. At that point you should have approximately 90% of your portfolio's total value in the stock market, and 10% in a gold mutual fund.[2] If the gold market continues to advance during a stock market crash, take the profits from the gold fund, and invest these profits in a good small stock mutual fund. (As a guide, study the section titled "The Hardest Hit Sectors of the Economy in a Depression With the Most Dynamic Recoveries".)

The Depression Part Of This Formula

Start taking profits as the market recovers.

For Example: Let's say that the Dow severely crashes during a severe recession, and it loses 90% from a high of 3000.

3000 x 90% = Dow 300

When the market starts to recover take the profits from the fund every time it advances 10% or more.

Fact: During a severe stock market crash, a 30 point to 90 point advance in the price of a stock or mutual fund can result in hundred's, if not thousand's, of percent in profits. For more details on this phenomenon, please refer to the reverse compounding table at the end of this book.

---

[1] By checking your financial statements every six months to a year.
[2] Make sure that the 10% is based on the highest total value of your portfolio just before the crash started to lower prices Use your financial statements as a reference.

$$3000 \times -90\% = \text{Dow } 300$$
$$3000 \times -80\% = \text{Dow } 600$$
$$3000 \times -70\% = \text{Dow } 900$$
$$3000 \times -60\% = \text{Dow } 1200$$
$$3000 \times -50\% = \text{Dow } 1500$$
$$3000 \times -40\% = \text{Dow } 1800$$
$$3000 \times -30\% = \text{Dow } 2100$$
$$3000 \times -20\% = \text{Dow } 2400$$
$$3000 \times -10\% = \text{Dow } 2700$$

The aggressive mutual fund system applies the above feature by continually re-investing and compounding new profits whether the market accelerates or declines.

What Makes These Two Systems Superior To Conventional Methods Of Investing?

Here are five good reasons:

No. 1   When stock market prices rise, the stock fund will generate greater profits, enabling the investor to pick up additional shares of a gold mutual fund at lower price levels *(i.e., gold prices often drop when the stock market rises).*

No. 2   When gold accelerates in price during an economic crisis, the profits can be used to purchase stock mutual funds at greatly reduced prices.

No. 3   Most of the cash in the money market account will continue to earn interest until the stock or bond market drops in price.

No. 4   The Gold System can act as a cushion for the losses acquired in a stock market crash.

No. 5   Profits from the stock or gold system are efficiently re-cycled during each succeeding crash.

Why Not Use A Dollar Cost Averaging Plan Instead?

Author's note:

Most of the dollar-cost averaging plans I had a chance to review at the university libraries only returned 55%–95% during the last 25 years. (This return barely kept up with the effects of taxes or inflation.)

Now, I would like to ask the reader one question: How can anyone expect to do better than the averages, when everyone invests the same way?[1]

---

[1]An enormous number of investors either subscribe to dollar cost averaging plans on a monthly basis, or invest at the wrong time on a long term basis. Each procedure guarantees mediocre investment results.

The Extreme Limitations Of
Dollar Cost Averaging

During the last two centuries the stock market has been up 65% of the time and down 35% of the time.

This means that the typical dollar cost averaging plan buys too many shares when the market is up, and not enough shares when the market is down. For example, let's say that you invest in a monthly dollar cost averaging plan. Now, it doesn't matter whether the stock market goes straight up or straight down. You're simply paying to much for those shares in the long run.

Are Small Stock Funds Still
A Good Buy?

Purchase small cap mutual funds during a severe stock market crash, since this is the perhaps the only time they're worth buying. For example, one year after the market *recovered* in 1976, small cap stocks lost so much of their compounded growth rate that it didn't even pay to own them on a long-term basis. *(Because of government-imposed taxes and inflation.)*

Is The Stock Market Dead
In The United States?

What can the conservative investor do, short of revolution?

Let's say that the Bond and Income System in Chapter IV generates the following returns during the next 10 years.[1]

Year 1.   8%
Year 2.   7%
Year 3.   6%
Year 4.   7%
Year 5. 30%
Year 6.   8%
Year 7.   7%
Year 8.   6%
Year 9. 15%
Year 10. 6%

A $10,000 investment grew into $26,000 or 10% compounded.

Keep your money in a good-paying money market account until the bond market crashes (a period associated with higher interest rates). Then slowly switch back from a long-term bond fund into a money market fund as interest rates decline. Follow the procedure on the next page so that you can substantially increase the return from your income investments.

---

[1]Between the 1980's and 1990's, money markets earned 12.8% compounded annually.

If the investor switches from a bond fund to a stock fund during a severe stock market crash,[1] and the mutual fund makes 50% during the eleventh year, the compounded rate of growth will have increased from 10% to 13.8%. Since the long term averages for the stock market have been around 9% to 10%, this method of investment has dramatically increased the total return of the portfolio by nearly three percentage points. From then on the income investor should use the aggressive mutual fund system in order to keep the compounded rate of growth at the 13.8% or above level. [2]

Why Should The Investor Consider The Above Strategy?

The government controls the biggest market for debt in the world. When the Fed needs additional funding to manage its deficits, it has no choice but to raise interest rates in order to attract foreign and domestic buyers. If the Fed raises interest rates to 14% on its Treasury issues, then corporations must offer 15% to 16% on their bonds to compete against the government. This ultimately stalls growth in every sector of the economy until Uncle Sam Inc. collects enough capital to stay in business.

The future of the U.S. economy doesn't look very bright, since slow growth, tax increases, unpredictable bouts of inflation, and massive Federal deficits have continually undermined the integrity of the financial system.

The most conservative investors should invest in bonds until the stock market totally collapses.

International Investors

While you're waiting for the U.S. stock market to collapse, don't ignore strong economies like Japan, Germany, and others that have lost 40% to 90% of their value in a crash. Take advantage of these markets with 10%–20% of your investment capital.

For Example: During the 1987 crash, the Mexico fund lost eighty to ninety percent of its value very quickly. If investors had placed five to ten percent of their portfolio in this fund, four years later their investment would have returned 1500%–1800%![3]

Question: What would happen if the investor had nine bad investments and one good one like the Mexico fund?

---

[1]When the Dow has lost 40% or more from its all time high, and small cap mutual funds have lost 55% to 70% of their value.
[2]Also refer to the "Bond and Income" chapter for more details on this subject.
[3]Before you make such an investment, size up the future value of the country you're investing in. I had a good idea that the U.S. Government wasn't about to let Mexico go down the drain since many U.S. manufacturers have profitable business down there. Mexico became a political play concerning U.S. jobs. In fact, in 1988 the U.S. government sent additional aid to Mexico because of the political fear that U.S. manufacturers would be hurt in a further collapse of the economy.

Answer: Let's say that the investor starts out with ten investments in ten diversified stocks, each investment equaling 10% of the portfolio's total value (this could include some severely undervalued closed-end funds or stocks).

Now, all nine of these investments manage to lose 50% of their value. Fortunately, one so-called dog returned 1000% (like the Mexico fund). That means that the investor still made a 45% profit from his/her investment.

The Profit Potential And Safety Of The Aggressive Mutual Fund System

(A stock portfolio or closed-end fund may be used instead of a mutual fund.)

As an example, the stock market system on the next page was tested against two of the biggest stock market crashes of this century:

• The Dow Jones Industrial Averages were used in this example for the first 6 years.

• In the last four years we used an aggressive growth fund that lost 70% of its value in a severe crash.

• The investment strategy coming up was designed to give the stock market investor a 14% to 15% compounded return over time.

The Stock Market System For The 1990's And Beyond.

The stock market system on the following page is an excellent example of The Aggressive Mutual Fund Trading System.

Question: What in the world do I need another investment strategy for; aren't there enough already?

Answer: Of course there are, but do any of them *really* work after taxes and inflation?

• There have been seven stock market declines since the 1960's when the stock market as a whole lost 27% or more of its value. During this period the average stock lost between 40% to 70% of its value.

• From 1940–1991 the long-term buy and hold investor was victimized by government inflationary policies, as nearly 85% of their investment capital was wiped out from taxes and inflation.

The primary advantage of the system on the next page is its ability to conserve capital for an unforeseen event, and to utilize it at its maximum profit potential.

The System In Action:

A $100,000 Account

FIRST YEAR (Small Crash)

A Ten-Year Investment Cycle Including A Four Year Depression.

During the first year the Dow drops 20%. Then shortly after the recovery, it gains an additional 10%. Formula: 40% of $100,000 comes to $40,000. Later in that same year, the Dow advances another 15% and the aggressive small stock mutual fund (or sector funds) advance 20% to 25% in value.

A profit of $10,000 is collected from the stock fund.
($40,000 x 25% = $10,000)

The $10,000 profit is moved into the appropriate money market funds. $8000 to *Money Market No. 1* (the stock fund). And $2,000 to *Money Market No. 2* (the gold money market fund).

The market goes up an additional 10% and the fund accumulates a profit of $4,000 [from the $40,000 remaining in the stock market.] *(This is also switched into the money market funds.)*

Total profits from the stock fund: $10,000 + 4,000 = $14,000

The other $60,000 is in money markets one and two earning 8% interest.
$60,000 x 8% = $4,800

Total profit: $10,000 + 4,000 + 4,800 = $18,800 or a 18.8% return on a $100,000 investment. Total value at the end of the first year = $118,800

Compounded return for the first year = 18.8%.

SECOND YEAR

During the second year the stock fund advances 30%.
$40,000 x 30% = $12,000

Plus the interest acquired on each money market fund at 7% interest.
$77,000 x 7% = $5,390

Total profits for the second year = $12,000 + $5,390 = $17,390

The total for the second year comes to $17,390. [An additional 14.8% gain from the first year's total of $118,800.]

The total profit at the end of the second year
$100,000 + $18,800 + $17,390 = $136,190
(36.1% for two years.)

Compounded return for the second year = 16.7%.

THIRD YEAR

In the third year the stock market advances 10% and the system accumulates 5% from the stock fund.

$40,000 x 5% = $2,000

Plus interest on the two money market funds $96,190 x 7% = $6,733.

Profits = $2,000 + $6,733 = $8,733

Profits for the third year = $8,733

Profits from the first and second year = $36,190

Total profits at the end of the third year.
$100,000 + $36,190 + $8,733 = $144,923

Compounded return for the third year = 13.1%.

FOURTH YEAR (SMALL CRASH)

In the fourth year the Dow drops 20%, then recovers; plus, the mutual fund accumulates an additional 10% profit. *Formula:* 40% of $144,923 comes to $57,969 [we still have $40,000 invested in the stock market from the first year]. Subtract $57,969 from $40,000 and add $17,969 to a brand new stock market fund. The $17,969 makes 20% in profit.

Profit on the $17,969 = $3,593

The $57,969 makes an additional 10% gain for a total of $5,796

The $86,954 in the money markets returns, [at 8% interest] = $6,956

Profits = $3,593 + $5,796 + $6,956 = $16,345

The total value of the portfolio at the end of the fourth year = $161,268 or 61.2%.

Compounded return for the forth year = 12.7%.

FIFTH YEAR

The Dow sets a new high with a 47% gain, while 40% of the portfolio ($57,969) remain in stocks from the previous year.

Profit from the 40% rise:
$57,969 x 40% = $23,187

The interest was added in from the balance of both money market accounts.
$103,299 x 7% interest = $7,230.

The total profits from this year are $23,187 + $7,230 = $30,417
Total profits from the last four years were $161,268
The total for five years = $191,685 Or 88.7%

Compounded return for the fifth year = 14%.

SIXTH YEAR

The market continues to recover and the mutual fund makes an additional 20% profit. Forty percent of the portfolio ($57,969) remains in stocks from the previous year.

Profit from the 20% gain:
$57,969 x 20% = $11,593

The interest was added in from the remaining balance of the combined money market accounts ($133,716).
At 7% interest = $9,360.

The total profits from the sixth year = $11,593 + $9,360 = $20,953
The total profits from the last five years were $191,685
The total for six years = $212,638 Or 119.4%

Compounded return for six years = 13.4%.

The system was put to the final test in a fund that lost 70% of its value during the 1973–1975 bear market. The only other crash that can compare with this one was the 1929–1932 crash. (Stocks lost 90% of their value between 1929-1932.)

SEVENTH YEAR
1972–1973

In the seventh year the Dow drops 24%.

Formula: 40% of $212,638 = $85,055
$57,969 remains in the stock market from the sixth year.
Subtract $85,055 from $57,969, and add $27,086 to a brand new stock fund.

We didn't make a profit from the stock market this year.

However, the money market funds returned:
$127,583 x 8% = $7,200.

The total for the seventh years equals:

$212,638 + $7,200 = $219,838

EIGHT YEAR, DEPRESSION LIKE CRASH

1973–74 (The Dow lost 45% of its value during this period).

The remaining capital from *Money Market No. 1* was placed in the stock fund.

Money Market No. 2 was added to the stock fund as well as most of the gold account.

The money market funds accumulate $500 in profit during this period.

NINTH AND TENTH YEARS

1975 to December 31, 1976
The fund fully recovers from the crash in 1977
(Four years from the start of a severe bear market.)

What did the fund return when it finally broke even in January 1977?

First, the $86,930 from *Money Market No. 1* returned 85%,
for a profit of $73,890

And, second, the $43,465 in *Money Market No. 2* returned 115%,
for a profit of $45,584

The sixth year turned out to be the last profitable year for the stock fund.
Total profits during this period = $217,327.

For The Seventh, Eight, Ninth, And Tenth Years

The aggressive mutual fund system made a profit of $90,315.

The total investment return for ten years:
$217,327 + $119,474 = $336,801 (Or 236% profit for a miserable ten-year period.)

In ten depression-like years this system returned 13% on a compounded basis, while the lump-sum investor's return fell to 9% for the same 10-year period.

If you're nervous about another crash phase, sell your mutual fund and buy a well managed closed-end fund. Set trailing stop losses on it until it hits the 14%-or-over compounded level. At that point, let 40% of your total portfolio's value remain in the market and start from there. (Follow the Chapter V Supplement proceeding this chapter as a guide to any changes that may occur in the long term cycle.)

A fine return, considering that the fund lost over 70% of its value during the last four years. Keep in mind that gold and bond prices went through the roof during the 1970's as well as the 1930's Great Depression era. So this return actually understates the true profit potential of this system.

This stock market system in no way resembles a balanced mutual fund. Historically speaking, the top returns from balanced mutual funds have been 6% to 8% over the long term.

Adding The Profit Potential From The Gold System
Between 1970-1980 gold mutual funds returned 31% compounded.[1]

If we add in the beneficial effects from the Gold System to the stock market system, the overall return from the previous stock market example will improve dramatically. For example, since the total for 10 years was $336,801, a ten year annualized 20% return from the gold system will increase the total return of the portfolio to 16.5% annually. At the low end of the scale, if the investor only manages to accumulate a 10% annual gain from the gold system, this will still increase the total return of the portfolio to 14.5% (after) a severe economic crisis has elapsed.

Historical Fact:
During the terrible 1970's, only a very few top performing mutual funds returned 12% on a annual basis. Most funds declined to a 7% compounded level.

How did the stock market system compare to the lump sum investor?
The First year he lost -17 but the market came back 27% = +7% gain
The Second year he made +30% gain
The Third year he broke even
The Fourth year he lost 20% but gained 30% = +5% gain
The Fifth year he made 40%
The Sixth year he made 20%
The Seventh, Eight, Ninth, and Tenth Years he broke even.

During a 10-year period, the lump sum investor turned $100,000 into $257,641. Consequently, the aggressive mutual fund system turned $100,000 into $336,801, for an extra gain of $79,160.[2] *(Again, this amount understates the appreciable profits from the Gold System, the bond system, and the anti-climatic effect on pages 73-74).*

In order for the lump sum investor to regain a 14% compounded level, he/she will need the following returns after the fund breaks even from the crash:

65% gain during the 11th year to catch up with us, or a
37% compounded return for two years.
29% compounded return for three years.
25% compounded return for four years.
23% compounded return for five years.

---

[1]Unfortunately, this meant that the investor had to buy and sell at the perfect time.

Unless you're the new Warren Buffett in town, forget about trying to make returns like these. (The market will not accommodate you.) Review the stock market crashes in Chapter I. Try to find a period of time right after a severe crash when the stock market continued to make substantial gains without a downturn.[1]

The Startling Difference Between 9% Compounded And 14% Compounded

15 Years at:	9% =	$36,400
15 Years at:	14% =	$71,379
20 Years at:	9% =	$56,044
20 Years at:	14% =	$137,434
25 Years at:	9% =	$142,108
25 Years at:	14% =	$264,619
30 Years at:	9% =	$132,676
30 Years at:	14% =	$509,501
35 Years at:	9% =	$204,139
35 Years at:	14% =	$981,000
40 Years at:	9% =	$314,044
40 Years at:	14% =	$1,888,835
50 Years at:	9% =	$743,575
50 Years at:	14% =	$7,002,329

The Lump Sum Investor Versus The Stock Market System
A study in comparison.

- The stock market system started out with 40% invested in stocks, reserving 60% of the portfolio for a severe stock market crash. Both investors made 13% compounded annually for the first six years; unfortunately, the lump sum investors compounded return dropped significantly during the last four years.

- The Master Portfolio System in this chapter also eliminated a considerable amount of the risk associated with stock ownership during a severe crash.

---

[1]When the losses that occur from mutual fund expense fees are added in, the overall return will drop to 7%–8% on an annualized basis. Also the effects of taxation and inflation have not been figured into the above return.

The Gold System made outstanding gains during the 1970's and the 1930's Great Depression era (even though we didn't include them in the original ten-year stock market example).

The Cheapest Brokerages In America
Will your broker make you broker?

Deep Discount Brokerages can be a full 70% cheaper than full commissioned brokerages.

K. Aufhauser & Co. rates are the lowest in the U.S. Their prices are as follows:

For 100 to 200 shares, $25 commission to buy in, $25 commission to sell out.

For 500 shares, $40 in and $40 out.
Telephone number 1-800-368-3668.

Pacific Brokerage:

Pacific Brokerages has five locations throughout the continental United States, and their commission rates are also the lowest in the financial industry:

300 shares or under: $28 to buy in, and $28 to sell out of a stock. Their telephone number is 1-800-421-8395.

How Much Money Do You Need To Start An Affordable Stock Portfolio?
At least $40,000 dollars.

Good question. Figuring ten stocks in a portfolio,[1] and using the aforementioned K. Aufhauser & Co. as an example, a $40,000 portfolio with ten stocks traded just once would cost the investor an average of 1.25% a year.

In many instances, mutual funds are cheaper if they allow unlimited trading, and lower expense fees. However, if the investor rarely trades stocks, and understands what he/she is doing, then this method may be appropriate for them.

When Should I Begin Trading Stocks?
If you trade like most people, never!

Question: What is paper trading?

Answer: Paper trading is the art of "buying" and "selling" a stock with no money down; in order to test your ideas without losing a bundle.

---

[1]Don't buy too many stocks. Twelve to fifteen, in twelve to fifteen different industries will suffice. Trying to keep track of 30, 60, or 200 stocks is impossible. The investor who has this many stocks has a jungle instead of a portfolio, because there simply isn't enough time to concentrate on the companies worth looking at.

Question: How do you test the results of paper trading?

Answer: Locate the financial section of a newspaper and write down ten of your favorite stock picks, then purchase a monkey and let him pick ten of *his* favorites. Repeat this procedure four or five times during an average ten-year period. If the monkey outperforms you, let him continue picking stocks on a regular basis. However, if you outperform the monkey, then congratulations are in order, since 95% of all the mutual funds, pension funds, and financial institutions in this country cannot. One last piece of advice: make sure that the stock market cycle selected for this test includes a severe recession or a depression. Why? Historically, the top investment advisors in this country have always landed on their butts during a severe recession or a depression.

While you're learning the art of paper trading, find a great mutual fund to invest in.

How To Use Real Estate To Pyramid Your Way To Wealth In The Stock Or Bond Markets

Real Estate Debt Is IN
Stock Market Margin Is OUT

What are the primary advantages of using real estate debt versus stock market margin?

Fact No 1: If the investor purchases a stock, bond, or gold mutual fund using *stock market margin,* when the price falls from $10 a share to $5, the investment is completely worthless.

Fact No 2: If a *mortgage borrower* buys into a well diversified mutual fund during a stock market crash, even if the fund loses 99% of its value, the investor will not lose a penny, since he/she has fifteen or more year to pay back the loan.[1]

Alternative: A long term real estate mortgage is perhaps the safest way to borrow, since this kind of loan has long-term safety factors built in, and special tax write-off features. *Just remember not to get carried away with this form of debt; use it wisely, and in a severe crash only.*

The ideas in this chapter were compiled from conversations with the world's greatest investors. Then these same ideas were condensed so that the reader could benefit from all the latest investment strategies and insights currently available.

---

[1] After the loan is secured, the investor must save enough money to cover at least two years of interest payments; this can be readily deposited in a money market account.

Chapter V Supplement

Second Investment Supplement to be used in conjunction
with the Aggressive Mutual Fund System from the previous chapter
(Chapter V)

The Long Term Super-Cycle

Question: What are long term investment cycles?

Answer: Long term cycles are periods in the economy and the stock market
when a prolonged upward or downward economic environment exists.

Question: How can the investor navigate these economic storms with the
strategies in this book?

Answer: By following the methods in this chapter, in conjunction with the
strategies in Chapter V.

Use This System After The Stock Market Has Undergone
A Medium Crash Phase Only (Dow falling 24% to 35%)

Warning: *Use this investment technique one time after such a crash occurs.*

Hint: Follow this method after the stock market has recently been through a
medium crash phase only (like 1900, 1909, 1962, 1977, 1987, etc.). In other
words, if the stock market has been through a brief period of moderately
extended price levels, then follow the procedure below.

When the Dow falls 17% or more from its all time high, invest 40% of your
portfolio's total value in the market.

When the Dow falls 24% or more, add another 10% of the entire
portfolio's value to the stock market. (Figure 10% based on the highest total
value of your portfolio just before the crash started to lower prices.) Use your
statements as a reference. Then as the Dow returns to its former high (or 5%
to 6% before the Dow's former high), sell your profits and reduce your stock
holdings to 40% at that time.

If the Dow falls below 35% or more, add everything except 10% of the
portfolio's total value, and let this remain in a gold mutual fund. (Again, figure
10% based on the highest total value of the portfolio just before the crash
started to lower prices.) Use your financial statements as a reference.

Attention: Real Estate Owners

Extremely sophisticated investors may borrow additional capital for the
purchase of mutual funds or sector funds during a crash. Please follow the
advice in Chapter V titled, "How You Can Use Real Estate to Increase Your
Profits in the Stock or Bond Markets."

Third Supplement

The Third Investment Supplement is to be used in conjunction with the Aggressive Mutual Fund System from the previous chapter (Chapter V)

Question: Is this method of long term cycle investing perfect?

Answer: Yes and no.

The primary advantage of this strategy is to avoid the biggest stock market crashes in history, and to concentrate on the booms that follow these periods. This new procedure will dramatically increase the overall profitability of your investment vehicle during these times. (Unfortunately, there may be another crash before the boom cycle actually begins, so don't panic; just remember that you avoided the biggest stock market crashes in history by utilizing the strategies in this book, and that alone will dramatically increase your chances at beating the market.)

Hint: Use this method after the stock market has recently been through a *severe crash phase* (like 1907, 1919, 1937, 1969–74.) In other words, if the Dow lost 35% of its value two or three times during the last five to ten years, then you may use this method in the next three to four stock market declines.

Directions: When the Dow falls 17% or more from its all time high, invest 40% of your total portfolio's value in the stock market.

When the Dow falls 22% or more, add another 20% of the entire portfolio's value to the stock market. [Figure 20% based on the highest total value of the portfolio just before the crash started to lower prices.] Use your statements as a reference. Then take profits 10% at a time.

If the Dow falls below 35% or more, add everything except 10% of the entire portfolio's value and let this remain in a gold mutual fund. (Figure 10% of the highest dollar value of the portfolio (just) before the crash started to lower prices.) Again, use your financial statements as a reference.

Attention Real Estate Owners

Extremely sophisticated investors may borrow additional capital for the purchase of mutual funds or sector funds during a crash. Please follow the advice in Chapter V titled, "How You Can Use Real Estate to Increase Your Profits in the Stock or Bond Markets."

Pay Special Attention To The Next Section
Lighten up before the grim reaper cometh!

The Anti-Climactic Effect
Use This System Along With The Aggressive Mutual Fund System

When the stock market returns 5% to 6% from its former record high, or stock PE ratio's have reached high valuation levels, the investor may switch from an aggressive mutual fund to a conservative fund with far less risk. In order to find a conservative fund that performs well in down markets, go to the library and ask the librarian for a copy of the *Forbes Annual Mutual Fund Survey*, look for a conservative fund that is rated A+ or A in down markets. (If you invest in closed-end funds or stocks instead of mutual funds, look for a beta that is .70 or below.)[1]

Oh, What A Difference
An Anti-Climax Can Make!

By following the strategies below, the investor **can make up to 75% more** *from his/her return.*

This is one of the greatest contrarian strategies ever devised; please use it with the strategies in Chapter V to achieve maximum profit potential from your investments.

- If the investor switches from an aggressive mutual fund into a conservative fund *right before a crash*, then switches back into the aggressive fund *during a crash*, the total return from the fund will improve dramatically.

- *For example:* If aggressive mutual fund A loses 50% of its value in a stock market crash, and conservative mutual fund B loses 20%, the conservative investor will need 25% to break even from the crash, while the aggressive investor will require 100% to fully recover. Since the smart investor used the anti-climatic effect below and switched into the fund that requires 100% to break even, he/she will make up to 75% more from the investment return. In contrast, the investor who did not used this strategy will just break even when the market recovers. (If this is somewhat confusing, study the Reverse Compounding Table in the back of this book.)

How To Invest Before And After
An Anti-Climax

If the market is approaching a major top:

- Switch 50% of the investment capital from your aggressive mutual fund to a conservative fund two times before the crash.

- Or, switch 35% of the investment capital from your aggressive mutual fund to the conservative mutual fund three times before a crash.

---

[1]Beta refers to market volitility. Since 1.0 is the average (like the S&P 500), a beta of 2.0 would mean that it has twice the volitility of the market, whereas a beta of .50 would mean half the volitility of the marketplace, or a conservative position.

If the market is approaching a low:
Do the opposite

- Switch 50% of the investment capital from your conservative fund to a small cap mutual fund two times before the market approaches a bottom.

- Or, switch 35% of the investment capital from your conservative fund to a small cap mutual fund three times before the market approaches a bottom.

Anyone using this technique should keep in mind that it may not work perfectly each and every time. However, the long-term benefits far outweigh the short term inaccuracies.

Author's personal note:

This investment strategy takes full advantage of the low PE effect by switching into the most undervalued areas of the economy during a crash. *(Historically, low PE stocks have had the highest compounded returns during the last century.)*

Special advice for investors purchasing foreign closed-end funds:

Since many foreign closed-end funds are sold on the N.Y.S.E., wait until the entire U.S. stock market crashes before purchasing closed-end funds on a foreign exchange. *(Even though prices from a foreign closed-end fund will appear to have bottomed out during a recession, a downturn in the U.S. stock market will send prices to even lower levels.)*

The ideas in this chapter were compiled from conversations with the world's greatest investors. Then these same ideas were condensed so that the reader could benefit from all the latest investment strategies and insights currently available.

Chapter VI
How To Invest In A Depression
Or An Economic Crisis

The Biggest Economic Disasters
In American History

Follow the ideas in this book before you become history's next victim.

During the past 15 years (1977–1992) the U.S. deficit has grown more in size than the previous 200 years of American history.

If the depression era of the 1930's had never come about, little if anything would have been known about the effects of such a disaster on the financial system or the stock market. This chapter will teach the investor how to spot undervalued areas of the economy that have the greatest potential for growth during the next recession or depression.

Dear Reader: Certain areas of the economy will always experience greater selling pressure during a panic or a crisis. Follow the timely rules below in order to profit from these inefficiencies as they occur.

Ask Yourself These Very Important Questions

* *Is this area of the economy a powerful driving force behind the economy?* In other words if the industry represents a significant portion of GNP, the politicians will have no choice but to stimulate these areas of the economy first.

* Is it severely undervalued because of panic selling or bad news?

* Is it essential to the health and well-being of the economy?

* Is it a powerful yet politically stable foreign country experiencing serious economic problems?

* Does Warren Buffett like it? *(Big Plus!)*

What Rebounds In A Great Depression

Let me prove to you right here and now that soda pop is the stock market's life blood.

The following table represents a compiled list of the hardest hit industrial sectors during the Great Depression era.

	Lost (1929–1932)	Recovered (1932–1936)
Paper[1]	94%	1000%
Machine Tools	95%	994%
Automobiles	88%	400%
Building Materials	87%	490%
Home Furnishings	85%	425%
Finance Companies	81%	660%
Soft Drinks	62%	550%

Source: S&P

---

[1] If you don't believe that paper is vital to the economy, consider that a recent economic report shows that each American uses 645 pounds of paper a year.

The safest way to acquire the previous industries are through the use of sector funds. Fidelity Investments has a wide variety to choose from. Call them at 1-800-544-8888, ask the representative for a complete prospectus plus the annual report on each the sector funds listed below.

- Select **Paper & Forest.** Concentrates on paper manufacturers and makers of all paper related products.

- Select **Construction & Housing.** This fund primarily invests in building materials and other home furnishing companies.

- Select **Industrials & Technologies.** Concentrates on industrial computers, machinery, equipment, tools, farm equipment, etc.

- Select **Automotive.** Invests in automotive companies and affiliated industries that sell automotive parts.

- Select **Savings & Loans.** Invests in the strongest S & L's and other finance institutions.

The Paper Industry Is Perhaps
The Most Important Sector Of The Economy

- Paper products are extremely sensitive to supply and demand factors. For example: The table from the previous page shows that the paper industry lost 95% of its value between 1929–1932, then as soon as the recovery began in 1933, paper stocks recorded gains of 1000% or more from their lows. The importance of this sector of the economy should not be overlooked, since everything in the world utilizes paper as part of its packaging.

For Example: boxes, letters, construction materials, newspapers, magazines, books, government papers, business documents, building materials, junk mail, etc.

- During a typical recession or depression, the automotive industry would experience a massive drop in car sales, since many buyers would avoid the purchase of a new car until economic conditions improved.

- Building materials, home furnishings, and finance company stocks are especially sensitive to an economic crisis. First-time home buyers will undoubtedly put off the purchase of a new home until economic conditions improve. Nevertheless, once the economy does improve, earnings in this sector of the economy will eventually lead to higher stock prices.

- Tobacco companies also prospered during the Great Depression era, as many continued to increase their earnings throughout the 1930's. Why? A depression has little effect on anyone with a nicotine addiction. (Look at companies that manufacture low-priced cigarettes, since their earning could dramatically improve in a recession or a depression.)

Stocks With The Best Returns In The Great Depression Era
Welcome to the United States, land of "The Pop Culture."
You can't keep soda pop from bubbling, even in a depression!

	Lost (1929–1932)	Recovered (1932–1936)
Soft Drinks	62%	560%

The above figure represents an increase of 385% in the stock price of soda pop *after* this industry fully recovered from its 62% loss at the start of the Great Depression. This unusually large return made soda pop one of the best performing sectors of the market along with gold stocks during the Great Depression era.

Question: Why did soda pop companies continue to outperform other industrial groups during the Great Depression?

Answer: Soda pop companies like Coke™ or Pepsi™ don't have to waste their money on advertising during an economic crisis, since they already have a well established product line. And, furthermore, soda pop is so cheap to make that the company can continue to lower its prices and still make a profit.

What If The Economy Experiences A Combination Of Inflation And Deflation?
Oh — you mean political double-talk? In that event, God help us all!

If the economy experiances cycles of inflation or deflation in the future, the three areas of the economy listed below will most likely benefit from this combination, *as long as the investor purchases them in a severe crash.*

• Select **Paper & Forest.** Concentrates its portfolio on paper manufacturers and makers of paper-related products.

• Select **Construction & Housing.** This sector fund invest in building materials and home furnishing companies.

• Select **Gold mutual funds**, closed end funds, or gold mining stocks.

Fidelity Investments has a annual prospectus on the above sector funds. Call them at 1-800-544-8888.

King Midas Is Here To Answer Your Most Passionate Question
Will gold buy me happiness in the next depression,
or will it lose its magical touch?

George Bernard Shaw once said: *"You have a choice between trusting the natural stability of gold and the honesty and intelligence of the members of government. And with all due respect to these people, I advise you, as long as the capitalist system exists, vote for gold as part of your holdings."*

Hardly Anyone Alive
Has Ever Experienced A Depression
Especially a Great Depression.

Unfortunately, this is the ONLY depression that the public ever refers to when the economy looks bad. If such an cataclysmic event were to take place today, gold would undoubtedly provide the greatest protection from monetary default in all of recorded history.

Owning Gold Bullion Is The
Wrong Way To Invest. Since When?
How about forever!

Choose a gold mutual fund that primarily invests in gold mining stocks and *not* the bullion. Why? Because gold bullion can be one of the riskiest way to invest during an economic crisis, since history has repeatedly demonstrated that once gold hoarding gets out of hand, the government steps in and makes the metal illegal to own.[1] Fortunately, gold mining companies continue to profit by exporting gold to other economies affected by the depression. One such company, Homestake Mining, continued to improve its earnings throughout the Great Depression era, even though gold was banned in the United States after 1934. (Study the Homestake Mining Tables at the end of this book for more details on the price relationship between gold the metal, versus gold the stock.)

Why Do Gold Mining Companies
Continue To Make A Profit When
The Government Bans The Ownership Of Gold?

No. 1   The government may become a big buyer of gold in order to stabilize the currency.

No. 2   Exports of gold to other countries increase because they fear a similar economic crisis.

No. 3   Seventy-two percent of gold sales come from jewelry-related products imported or exported.

---

[1]To prevent hoarding, the U.S. Government made gold ownership illegal in 1934. It also confiscated gold bullion and nuismatic coins in order to strengthen the weakened currency. In 1974, the U.S. Government lifted its restrictions off gold ownership and made the purchase of the metal legal for the first time since 1934.

One Last Argument For
Gold Stocks Rather Than Gold Itself

Direct ownership of gold in a busted economy should be avoided since no one can trade it for anything of value. The metal itself may become valueless in comparison with other essential commodities, such as food, soap or tobacco. (This happened to Japan in the late 1940's.)

Chapter VII
Give Praise To The Holy Bomb

Fact: Because Russia and the United States are defense-oriented societies, smaller countries like Japan, Germany, and others will continue to surpass the Superpowers in economic superiority.

In 1944, the United States rewrote the Japanese constitution preventing them from rebuilding a world-threatening military empire. Unfortunately, that didn't stop the Soviet Union or the United States from stockpiling thousands of nuclear weapons and spending themselves into bankruptcy. During this period, Japan concentrated its output on economic improvement, while the U.S. and the U.S.S.R. played the brilliant game of, "I'll bet we can build more nuclear weapons than you can!"

Ronald Reagan's defense policies further pushed the Russian economy into bankruptcy, even though all of the latest reports suggest that their society would have collapsed on its own within a decade or so. In light of these new developments, some financial experts are predicting a big boom for the U.S. stock market.[1] Unfortunately.

No. 1   The U.S. savings rate is extremely low in comparison with other countries.

No. 2   Capital gains taxes are the highest of any country in the world.

No. 3   State and local governments are nearly bankrupt, and taxes continue to rise across the board. (Including the new so-called "user taxes.")

No. 4   The Federal deficit is now projected at $5 trillion for 1995.

No. 5   The government continues to eliminate tax write-offs, causing a abnormal amount of stagnation in the economy.

No. 6   The United States has the highest amount of consumer debt in the world.

No. 7   The U.S. is currently undergoing the biggest banking crisis in recorded history, thanks to the brilliance of the Reagan administration.

No. 8   Even though inflation has subsided since the 1970's, the Federal deficits growth rate will undoubtedly cause a new round of higher inflation and taxation to occur in the future. For example, during the post World War II era, inflation kept on rising until it hit a new high in 1947.[2] This in turn wiped out a large portion of the dollar's value (45%) between 1940–1950. The same event could easily repeat itself in the 1990's since inflationary measures have often been used to squeeze out additional taxes before and after an economic crisis.

---

[1] Keep in mind that these people work for big financial firms which make billions of dollars in commissions.
[2] The government decided to handle the cost of the war the way it always does, by passing it on to the taxpayers in the form of higher taxes and inflation.

Will America Come Back With A Vengeance?

How can it, when Japan owns just about everything, and our Federal deficit is projected at $5 trillion in 1995? Let's face it, we lost the cold war. Remember the old saying, "We have seen the enemy, and it is ourselves." That saying was made for the 1990's and beyond.

Question: How will major wars be fought in the future?

Answer: World wars are now fought economically and this makes them far more dangerous then they were in the past. As soon as each superpower is finished with the ultimate weapon of destruction, they'll eventually dismantle their arsenals and move on to the next ultimate weapon of destruction.

Question: What about the length of time it takes to fight these new wars?

Answer: Perhaps the biggest problem associated with economic wars is that they take much longer than a normal war to end, since each side lets uncontrollable fears and anxieties build-up for greater lengths of time.[1]

Question: Isn't it true that Russia and the United States will soon dispose of their nuclear arsenals?

Answer: Unfortunately, this could be another form of political posturing [manure]. The U.S. is already replacing its nuclear arsenal with newer and more sophisticated weapons systems (Star Wars), and don't forget the *very real* possibility of other nations emerging as militaristic superpowers in the future. With people like Saddam Hussein around, the world is never going to be a safe place to live in, and the superpowers will have no choice except to maintain as much militaristic supremacy as possible.[2]

Question: Will the politicians ever find a way to balance the budget?

Answer: How can they, when they can't even balance their own checkbooks. All the bright ideas about value-added taxes, or tax cuts will accomplish nothing at this late stage. (In five thousand years of recorded history every economic power on earth failed to come up with a last minute solution to the problems that effected their economies).

Question: Why does the government fail to address serious economic issues like the Federal deficit?

Answer: Because politicians can't agree on anything except the size of their pay checks.

Question: Why is the government such a poorly run business?

Answer: As any competent business man knows, in order for a business to survive it must quickly eliminate the problems that threaten the company's future or be eliminated in the process (*i.e.,* too much debt, incompetent

---

[1]This can eventually lead to extreme economic disaster on a global scale.
[2]Remember, Superpowers have the idea that they are the protectors of the world. And this pompous thinking has constantly destroyed every major economic power throughout recorded history.

management, scandals, etc.) Unfortunately, the government always fails to address the problems of the economy until its too late, leaving two hundred and fifty million people (us!) paying for their mistakes.

Last Remarks: As long as the governments of the world continue to spend beyond their means, high inflation, excessive taxation, and runaway deficits will end in total economic disaster.

Very Last Remarks: Use the investment strategies in this book to protect your financial future from the very real possibility of a full scale economic crisis.

Reverse Compounding

If The Market Drops By This Amount	It Needs to Recover By This Amount to Break Even
10%	11.11%
15%	17.65%
20%	25.00%
25%	33.33%
30%	42.86%
35%	53.85%
40%	66.67%
45%	81.82%
50%	100.00%
55%	122.22%
60%	150.00%
65%	185.71%
70%	233.33%
75%	300.00%
80%	400.00%
85%	614.29%
87%	669.23%
88%	733.33%
89%	809.09%
90%	900.00%
91%	1011.11%
92%	1150.00%
93%	1328.57%
94%	1566.67%
95%	1900.00%
96%	2400.00%
97%	3233.33%
98%	4900.00%
99%	9900.00%

Homestake Mining Company
Weekly Stock Prices and Dow Jones Industrial Averages
1929

DATE	BID	ASK	CLOSE	Prices Adjusted for Stock Splits BID	ASK	CLOSE	DOW JONES	GOLD PRICE
04-Jan-29 F	75.000	78.000	76.500 *	0.391	0.406	0.398	0.00	20.67
11-Jan-29 F	75.000	76.000	75.500 *	0.391	0.396	0.393	0.00	20.67
18-Jan-29 F	75.500	76.000	75.750 *	0.393	0.396	0.395	0.00	20.67
25-Jan-29 F	73.500	74.500	74.000 *	0.383	0.388	0.385	0.00	20.67
01-Feb-29 F	73.500	73.750	73.625 *	0.383	0.384	0.383	0.00	20.67
06-Feb-29 F	73.250	73.500	73.375 *	0.382	0.383	0.382	301.53	20.67
15-Feb-29 F	72.000	74.000	73.000 *	0.375	0.385	0.380	0.00	20.67
21-Feb-29 Th	72.000	72.750	72.375 *	0.375	0.379	0.377	310.06	20.67
01-Mar-29 F	72.250	73.000	72.625 *	0.376	0.380	0.378		20.67
08-Mar-29 F	72.875	73.000	72.938 *	0.380	0.380	0.380	0.00	20.67
15-Mar-29 F	73.500	75.000	74.250 *	0.383	0.391	0.387	0.00	20.67
25-Mar-29 M	73.875	75.000	74.438 *	0.385	0.391	0.388	0.00	20.67
28-Mar-29 Th	73.250	73.375	73.313 *	0.382	0.382	0.382	308.85	20.67
05-Apr-29 F	72.500	73.500	77.250 *	0.378	0.383	0.402	0.00	20.67
12-Apr-29 F	72.500	73.500	75.000 *	0.378	0.383	0.391	0.00	20.67
19-Apr-29 F	73.000	73.375	75.000 *	0.380	0.382	0.391	0.00	20.67
26-Apr-29 F			75.000	0.000	0.000	0.391	0.00	20.67
03-May-29 F	76.125	76.500	76.000 *	0.396	0.398	0.396	0.00	20.67
10-May-29 F	75.250	76.500	75.875 *	0.392	0.398	0.395	0.00	20.67
17-May-29 F	76.250	76.875	76.563 *	0.397	0.400	0.399	0.00	20.67
24-May-29 F	76.250	76.875	76.563 *	0.397	0.400	0.399	0.00	20.67
31-May-29 F			76.00	0.000	0.000	0.396	0.00	20.67
07-Jun-29 F	73.000	75.500	74.250 *	0.380	0.393	0.387	0.00	20.67
14-Jun-29 F			73.000	0.000	0.000	0.380	0.00	20.67
21-Jun-29 F	70.250	73.000	71.625 *	0.366	0.380	0.373	0.00	20.67
28-Jun-29 F	71.000	72.000	77.000 *	0.370	0.375	0.401	0.00	20.67
05-Jul-29 F	72.000	73.000	72.500 *	0.375	0.380	0.378	0.00	20.67
12-Jul-29 F	72.000	73.000	72.500 *	0.375	0.380	0.378	0.00	20.67
19-Jul-29 F			73.500 *	0.000	0.000	0.380	0.00	20.67
26-Jul-29 F			75.000	0.000	0.000	0.391	0.00	20.67
02-Aug-29 F	74.000	76.000	78.000 *	0.385	0.396	0.406	0.00	20.67
09-Aug-29 F	75.000	75.750	75.375 *	0.391	0.395	0.393	0.00	20.67
16-Aug-29 F			93.000	0.000	0.000	0.409	0.00	20.67
23-Aug-29 F			93.000	0.000	0.000	0.484	0.00	20.67
30-Aug-29 F			80.000	0.000	0.000	0.417	380.33	20.67
06-Sep-29 F	80.000	88.000	84.000 *	0.417	0.458	0.438	0.00	20.67
13-Sep-29 F	79.000	89.000	79.000 *	0.411	0.464	0.412	0.00	20.67
20-Sep-29 F	85.000	88.500	86.500	0.443	0.461	0.451	0.00	20.67
27-Sep-29 F			86.500	0.000	0.000	0.451	0.00	20.67
04-Oct-29 F	85.000	87.500	86.250 *	0.443	0.456	0.449	0.00	20.67
11-Oct-29 F	84.500	86.000	85.250 *	0.440	0.448	0.444	352.69	20.67
18-Oct-29 F	84.500	85.000	82.000 *	0.440	0.443	0.427	0.00	20.67
25-Oct-29 F			83.500	0.000	0.000	0.435	0.00	20.67
01-Nov-29-F			76.000	0.000	0.000	0.396	0.00	20.67
08-Nov-29 F	70.500	75.000	72.750 *	0.367	0.391	0.379	236.53	20.67
15-Nov-29 F			65.000	0.000	0.000	0.339	228.73	20.67
22-Nov-29 F			74.000	0.000	0.000	0.385	0.00	20.67
27-Nov-29 W	80.000	95.000	87.500 *	0.417	0.495	0.456	238.95	20.67
06-Dec-29 F	80.000	88.000	84.000 *	0.417	0.458	0.438	0.00	20.67
13-Dec-29 F			80.000	0.000	0.000	0.417	0.00	20.67
20-Dec-29 F	77.000	80.000	78.500 *	0.401	0.417	0.409	0.00	20.67
27-Dec-29 F	77.000	80.000	78.500 *	0.401	0.417	0.409	0.00	20.67

Closing price not available. Closing price computed as average of bid and ask.

Homestake Mining Company
Weekly Stock Prices and Dow Jones Industrial Averages
1933

DATE	BID	ASK	CLOSE	BID	ASK	CLOSE	DOW JONES	GOLD PRICE
					Prices Adjusted for Stock Splits			
08-Jan-33 F			155.000	0.000	0.000	0.807	62.96	20.67
13-Jan-33 F			150.000	0.000	0.000	0.781	0.00	20.67
20-Jan-33 F			147.500	0.000	0.000	0.768	0.00	20.67
27-Jan-33 F	150.000	154.000	152.000 *	0.781	0.802	0.792	0.00	20.67
03-Feb-33 F			158.500	0.000	0.000	0.826	0.00	20.67
10-Feb-33 F			157.500	0.000	0.000	0.820	0.00	20.67
17-Feb-33 F	181.000	168.00	164.500 *	0.839	0.875	0.857	0.00	20.67
24-Feb-33 F			162.500	0.000	0.000	0.846	0.00	20.67
03-Mar-33 F			165.750	0.000	0.000	0.863	0.00	20.67
10-Mar-33 F	STOCK MARKET CLOSED		0.000	0.000	0.000	0.000	0.00	20.67
17-Mar-33 F			158.000	0.000	0.000	0.823	0.00	20.67
24-Mar-33 F			163.500 *	0.000	0.000	0.852	0.00	20.67
31-Mar-33 F	169.00	172.00	170.500 *	0.880	0.896	0.888	0.00	20.67
07-Apr-33 F			193.000	0.000	0.000	1.005	0.00	20.67
13-Apr-33 Th			189.000	0.000	0.000	0.984	0.00	20.67
21-Apr-33 F			199.625	0.000	0.000	1.040	0.00	20.67
28-Apr-33 F			185.000	0.000	0.000	0.964	0.00	20.67
05-May-33 F			185.500	0.000	0.000	0.966	0.00	20.67
12-May-33 F			193.000	0.000	0.000	1.005	0.00	20.67
19-May-33 F			192.000	0.000	0.000	1.042	0.00	20.67
26-May-33 F			200.000	0.000	0.000	1.042	0.00	20.67
02-Jun-33 F			230.000	0.000	0.000	1.196	0.00	20.67
09-Jun-33 F			244.750	0.000	0.000	1.275	0.00	20.67
16-Jun-33 F			220.000	0.000	0.000	1.146	0.00	20.67
23-Jun-33 F			228.000	0.000	0.000	1.188	0.00	20.67
30-Jun-33 F	220.00	230.00	225.000 *	1.146	1.198	1.172	0.00	20.67
07-Jul-33 F			236.000	0.000	0.000	1.229	0.00	20.67
14-Jul-33 F			235.000	0.000	0.000	1.224	0.00	20.67
21-Jul-33 F			230.000	0.000	0.000	1.198	0.00	20.67
28-Jul-33 F			235.000	0.000	0.000	1.224	94.54	20.67
04-Aug-33 F			220.000	0.000	0.000	1.146	92.62	20.67
11-Aug-33 F			245.000	0.000	0.000	1.276	97.47	20.67
18-Aug-33 F			260.000	0.000	0.000	1.354	98.32	20.67
25-Aug-33 F			294.000	0.000	0.000	1.531	105.07	20.67
01-Sep-33 F			303.000	0.000	0.000	1.578	103.66	20.67
08-Sep-33 F			300.000	0.000	0.000	1.563	0.00	20.67
15-Sep-33 F			325.000	0.000	0.000	1.693	0.00	20.67
22-Sep-33 F			358.000	0.000	0.000	1.865	0.00	20.67
29-Sep-33 F			341.000	0.000	0.000	1.776	0.00	20.67
05-Oct-33 Th			373.000	0.000	0.000	1.943	0.00	20.67
13-Oct-33 F			320.000	0.000	0.000	1.667	0.00	20.67
19-Oct-33 Th			303.000	0.000	0.000	1.576	0.00	20.67
27-Oct-33 F			361.000	0.000	0.000	1.880	0.00	20.67
03-Nov-33 F	320.000	324.000	322.000 *	1.667	1.688	1.677	0.00	20.67
10-Nov-33 F			320.000	0.000	0.000	1.667	0.00	20.67
17-Nov-33 F			326.000	0.000	0.000	1.696	0.00	20.67
24-Nov-33 F			304.000	0.000	0.000	1.583	0.00	20.67
01-Dec-33 F			306.000	0.000	0.000	1.594	0.00	20.67
08-Dec-33 F			310.000	0.000	0.000	1.615	0.00	20.67
15-Dec-33 F			315.000	0.000	0.000	1.641	0.00	20.67
22-Dec-33 F			300.000	0.000	0.000	1.563	0.00	20.67
29-Dec-33 F			315.000	0.000	0.000	1.641	0.00	20.67

Closing price not available. Closing price computed as average of bid and ask.

Homestake Mining Company
Weekly Stock Prices and Dow Jones Industrial Averages
1936

DATE	BID	ASK	CLOSE	BID	ASK	CLOSE	DOW JONES	GOLD PRICE
				Prices Adjusted for Stock Splits				

DATE	BID	ASK	CLOSE	Prices Adjusted for Stock Splits BID	ASK	CLOSE	DOW JONES	GOLD PRICE
03-Jan-36 F	480.000	550.000	515.000 *	2.500	2.865	2.682	144.69	35.00
10-Jan-36 F	503.000	530.000	516.500 *	2.620	2.760	2.690	147.08	35.00
17-Jan-36 F	500.000	520.000	510.000 *	2.604	2.708	2.656	145.81	35.00
24-Jan-36 F	510.000	540.000	525.000 *	2.658	2.813	2.734	146.59	35.00
31-Jan-36 F	495.000	529.000	512.000 *	2.578	2.755	2.667	149.49	35.00
07-Feb-36 F	500.000	525.000	512.500 *	2.604	2.734	2.669	150.17	35.00
14-Feb-36 F	525.000	530.000	527.500 *	2.734	2.760	2.747	151.97	35.00
20-Feb-36 Th	521.000	534.750	527.875 *	2.714	2.785	2.749	154.43	35.00
28-Feb-36 F	505.000	529.000	517.000 *	2.630	2.755	2.693	152.53	35.00
06-Mar-36 F	480.000	520.000	500.000 *	2.500	2.708	2.604	158.75	35.00
13-Mar-36 F	450.000	495.000	472.500 *	2.344	2.578	2.461	150.42	35.00
20-Mar-36 F	430.000	490.000	460.000 *	2.240	2.552	2.396	157.42	35.00
27-Mar-36 F	450.000	490.000	470.000 *	2.344	2.552	2.448	155.52	35.00
03-Apr-36 F	470.000	500.000	485.000 *	2.448	2.604	2.526	160.09	35.00
09-Apr-36 Th	430.000	490.000	460.000 *	2.240	2.552	2.396	160.25	35.00
17-Apr-36 F	440.000	490.000	465.000 *	2.292	2.552	2.422	157.78	35.00
24-Apr-36 F	451.000	499.000	475.000 *	2.349	2.599	2.474	151.54	35.00
01-May-36 F	450.000	499.000	474.500 *	2.344	2.599	2.471	147.07	35.00
08-May-36 F	461.000	498.000	479.500 *	2.401	2.594	2.498	146.87	35.00
15-May-36 F	455.000	484.000	469.500 *	2.370	2.521	2.445	151.60	35.00
22-May-36 F	460.000	484.000	472.000 *	2.396	2.521	2.458	149.58	35.00
28-May-36 Th	463.000	480.000	471.500 *	2.411	2.500	2.456	151.77	35.00
05-Jun-36 F	455.000	480.000	467.500 *	2.370	2.500	2.435	149.26	35.00
12-Jun-36 F	451.000	470.000	460.500 *	2.349	2.448	2.396	153.71	35.00
19-Jun-36 F	450.000	470.000	460.000 *	2.344	2.448	2.396	156.53	35.00
26-Jun-36 F	427.125	460.000	443.563 *	2.225	2.396	2.310	158.21	35.00
03-Jul-36 F	415.000	427.000	421.000 *	2.161	2.224	2.193	158.11	35.00
10-Jul-36 F	410.000	430.000	420.000 *	2.135	2.240	2.188	160.07	35.00
17-Jul-36 F	330.000	420.000	375.000 *	1.719	2.188	1.953	163.55	35.00
24-Jul-36 F	411.000	450.000	430.500 *	2.141	2.344	2.242	164.37	35.00
31-Jul-36 F	411.000	430.000	420.500 *	2.141	2.240	2.190	164.86	35.00
07-Aug-36 F	425.000	430.000	427.500 *	2.214	2.240	2.227	168.01	35.00
14-Aug-36 F	420.000	450.000	435.000 *	2.188	2.344	2.266	165.75	35.00
21-Aug-36 F	420.000	440.000	430.000 *	2.188	2.292	2.240	160.80	35.00
28-Aug-36 F	425.000	435.000	430.000 *	2.214	2.266	2.240	166.78	35.00
04-Sep-36 F	426.000	434.000	430.000 *	2.219	2.260	2.240	167.04	35.00
11-Sep-36 F	429.000	448.000	438.500 *	2.234	2.333	2.284	168.59	35.00
18-Sep-36 F	427.000	444.000	435.500 *	2.224	2.313	2.268	167.76	35.00
25-Sep-36 F	403.000	432.000	417.500 *	2.099	2.250	2.174	166.36	35.00
02-Oct-36 F	423.000	430.000	426.500 *	2.203	2.240	2.221	170.76	35.00
09-Oct-36 F	410.000	428.000	419.000 *	2.135	2.229	2.182	175.19	35.00
16-Oct-36 F	404.000	425.000	414.500 *	2.104	2.214	2.159	176.66	35.00
23-Oct-36 F	416.000	425.000	420.500 *	2.167	2.214	2.190	175.60	35.00
30-Oct-36 F	410.000	420.000	415.000 *	2.135	2.188	2.161	177.15	35.00
06-Nov-36 F	420.000	434.000	427.000 *	2.188	2.260	2.224	181.60	35.00
13-Nov-36 F	440.000	454.000	447.000 *	2.292	2.365	2.328	182.24	35.00
20-Nov-36 F	417.000	470.000	443.500 *	2.172	2.448	2.310	180.74	35.00
27-Nov-36 F	420.000	470.000	445.000 *	2.188	2.448	2.318	182.81	35.00
04-Dec-36 F	425.000	444.000	434.500 *	2.214	2.313	2.263	180.97	35.00
11-Dec-36 F	410.000	443.000	426.500 *	2.135	2.307	2.221	181.10	35.00
18-Dec-36 F	405.000	434.000	419.500 *	2.109	2.260	2.185	179.42	35.00
24-Dec-36 Th	400.000	420.000	410.000 *	2.083	2.188	2.135	0.00	35.00
31-Dec-36 Th	405.000	439.000	422.000 *	2.109	2/286	2.198	197.90	35.00

*Closing price not available. Closing price computed as average of bid and ask.